FAR OUT

THE DAWNING

of

NEW AGE BRITAIN

To my mother Monique Lentier
Miriam Akhtar

To the memory of my dear spiritualist mother
Marjorie Humphries (1924-1992)
Steve Humphries

FAR OUT

THE DAWNING OF NEW AGE BRITAIN

Miriam Akhtar & Steve Humphries

with Lucy Swingler

Sansom &
Company

in association with
Channel Four Television

First published in 1999 by Sansom & Company Ltd.,
81g Pembroke Road, Bristol BS8 3EA

This book has been published to accompany the series of television
programmes of the same name produced by Testimony Films for
Channel Four Television.

ISBN 1 900178 22 2

British Library Cataloguing in Publication Data
A catalogue record for this book is available from
The British Library.

Designed and typeset by Gendall Design, Falmouth and printed by
Bookcraft Ltd, Midsomer Norton.

CONTENTS

INTRODUCTION

THE New Age is an enigma. It first seemed to emerge in Britain in the 1960s along with flower power, hippies and the counter culture. At its heart was a search for personal spiritual meaning, very different to anything on offer from the established church. It looked to the mystic East and the pagan past for spiritual inspiration. Most critics saw this spiritual quest as a passing fashion that would soon vanish without trace. But by the 1980s the New Age movement had become firmly entrenched, with Glastonbury the main place of pilgrimage. More surprisingly the whole panoply of New Age beliefs – yoga, ley lines, aromatherapy, alternative medicine, natural healing, channelling, past life regression, crystal power and even fairies – were being taken more seriously. Some became part of mainstream culture with crystal shops in almost every new shopping centre and 'mind, body, spirit' books amongst the nation's bestsellers. The buzzword of the nineties was spirituality.

To most observers the New Age marked a sea change in British history and culture, separating the younger generation from the church going, sensible men and women of times past. In fact it has a long history going back to the turn of the century and beyond. There is nothing new about the New Age. Mysticism first became fashionable during the 1920s with the teachings of the young Indian guru Krishnamurti. Spiritualism enjoyed its hey-day during the Second World War. Back-to-the-land communes, some of which experimented with free love, were far more prevalent in the 1920s than in the 1960s. We also led the world in our obsession with astrology during the Depression years of the 1930s. Britain, despite its reputation for conservatism and conventionality, was an early pioneer of New Age think-ing. This is the paradox that this book and the television series it accompa-nies try to unravel. It is an exploration of the origins and hidden history of the New Age movement in Britain. For us it has been a fascinating histori-cal and spiritual journey.

There have been a number of autobiographies and biographies of the most influential New Age thinkers in Britain. Colourful and extrovert char-acters like Madame Blavatsky, the founder of the influential Theosophical Society, Rudolph Steiner, the pioneer of Anthroposophy and Waldorf Schools, and Gerald Gardner who reinvented the pagan religion of wicca or witchcraft have all received attention. But we know almost nothing about the followers and devotees of these early alternative spiritual movements. Who were the men and women who joined occult and pagan groups, dropped out to form communes, attended seances and experimented with alternative life styles? What were their hopes and fears, their passions and their loves? What were their social origins and their family background? Did they face social rejection for their beliefs? Did they try to keep them secret? Did they find fulfilment in their quest for spiritual meaning outside the established church or did it all end in disillusionment? What ideas and ideals did they share with the New Age movement of today?

There is little or no documentary evidence that could begin to answer these and our many other questions. We realised two years ago when this project began that living memory would provide the bedrock of our histo-ry. We would need to trace the last survivors of early New Age Britain. If they were alive, most would now be in their eighties and nineties. We urgently contacted every New Age organisation, magazine and journal to tap into their network of older members. We placed letters in local news-papers throughout Britain calling for the memories of early mystics, spiri-tualists and pagans. And we visited New Age centres like Glastonbury and the Findhorn community on the remote north east coast of Scotland. The response we received has been warm and extremely generous. It has enabled us to track down and interview some extraordinary men and women with stories that would otherwise never have been known. Those involved with the New Age movement today seem anxious that their history should be documented and that the memories of the men and women who took the road less travelled during the first half of the century should not be lost.

We discovered and spoke to around three hundred people scattered all over Britain in the course of our research. Of these we completed pilot interviews with more than sixty. Those we felt were most interesting were interviewed in depth for the television programmes and the book. We chose them because of the vividness of their memories and their ability to illustrate a broad spectrum of New Age experience and belief. Many had not spoken openly about their lives before. Often nobody had thought to ask them. More important, some felt they would not be taken seriously and would be ridiculed for ideas that were out of step with their time. Here they tell their stories in their own words, sometimes for the first time. We hear the voice of some of our oldest commune dwellers, mystics, white witches, spiritualists, naturists, astrologers, vegetarians and organic farmers, now in their seventies, eighties and nineties. They re-create in fascinating detail the birth of the New Age in pre-war Britain.

The book is organised into six chapters each one exploring a key theme in the development of New Age Britain. They feature the influence of eastern mysticism, paganism, spiritualism, alternative life styles, experimental communities and end-of-the-world movements. Each chapter begins with a historical introduction, sketching the background to the testimonies that follow.

A few of the beliefs once held by our interviewees are self-evidently false. History has proved them wrong, most obviously the predictions for the end of the world in 1914 and 1973. Others claim to have had spiritual and mystical experiences, the authenticity of which some readers may question. However, we make no general attempt to scrutinise the truth of such experiences and beliefs. Instead our purpose is to document their existence and show how they came to play so important a role in the lives of British people in the twentieth century.

Many New Age beliefs were in fact rediscovered at a particular historical moment. The passion for astrology with its mystical predictions first emerged during the inter-war years depression when there was great uncertainty about the future. Spiritualism enjoyed its finest hour during the two world wars when people looked for comfort to help cope with the death of loved ones. And 'end of time' prophecies had most appeal at times of national crisis, especially during the cold war era with the threat of nuclear war. Beliefs like these seemed to answer a spiritual need that was beyond the bounds of conventional religion.

Perhaps the most constant feature of New Age Britain has been its reversal of the balance of power between the sexes. It allowed women to exercise spiritual power as mediums, healers and visionaries at a time when the idea of women priests was ridiculed. It celebrated qualities regarded as female like instinct, imagination and feeling above established values of patriarchy and masculinity. Its empowerment of women was reflected in the fact that the majority of those who embraced New Age and alternative beliefs during the first half of the century were women.

THE CALL
OF THE EAST

CHAPTER ONE

IN the 1920s young people all over Britain flocked to see Krishna-murti, the first Indian guru to achieve mass appeal in the West. He was heralded as the new messiah who would bring a new era of peace and harmony of man with nature. Thousands fervently believed that his incarnation marked the beginning of a New Age – the Age of Aquarius. But in 1929 he dramatically renounced his title of Messiah – the pressure had been too much for him. His rise to fame was part of a broader trend for the mystic East was one of the great sources of spiritual inspiration for the early New Age movement in Britain.

The ancient Hindu and Buddhist religions held a deep fascination for the western seeker of truth. In an age of Empire when Britain despatched an army of Christian missionaries to convert the heathen all over the world, there were also a forgotten few who looked to the East with respect. In fact it was through the Empire that many were first introduced to eastern religion. Amongst the pioneers of the New Age were the wives of expatriates.

The most influential movement that introduced the mystic traditions of the east to Britain was theosophy. (Theosophy is a Greek word which means wisdom of God) The Theosophical Society was formed in 1875 by

BELOW
Jiddu Krishnamurti's teachings inspired thousands of theosophical followers.

OPPOSITE
Ranchor Prime joined the first Krishna temple in London.

Madame Blavatsky, a renegade and much travelled Russian aristocrat who wrote two landmark books *Isis Unveiled* (1877) and *The Secret Doctrine* (1888). She broke the mould of Christian thinking which had claimed a monopoly of spiritual truth.

Blavatsky was the first to popularise the Hindu idea of reincarnation in the west. She claimed that Darwin was wrong and that man was descended not from apes but from spirit beings. For her there was a divine plan of which every individual formed a part. The key to life and the universe was the spiritual progression of individuals through constant death and re-birth towards a state of perfection. This spiritual journey began thousands of years ago in lost civilizations like Atlantis. According to Blavatsky the human race was fast approaching a New Age of love and cosmic consciousness in which people would be aware of their previous incarnations and the meaning of life would become clear.

Blavatsky died in 1891 but theosophy was revitalised in Britain by the feminist campaigner Annie Besant who became one of the leading figures in the Theosophical Society. It influenced literary figures like Oscar Wilde, W.B. Yeats, George Bernard Shaw and Aldous Huxley. By the first decades of the century its mystical ideals began to penetrate middle-class Britain, with a special appeal for women and young people.

Theosophists believed the Hindu doctrine of avatars which held that God incarnated himself when it was necessary to advance evolution. The Society, assuming that the world was on the verge of a New Age, began searching for one. In 1908 an Indian boy, Jiddu Krishnamurti, who had what was thought to be an exceptional aura, was spotted by theosophists swimming in a river close to the world headquarters of the Theosophical Society in Adyar. He was groomed to be the new world teacher and became the first Indian guru to attract a cult following in Britain. In 1911 the Theosophical Society proclaimed that Krishnamurti was a channel for the wisdom of the Lord Maitreya, the last incarnation of the Buddha. In the following decades his books, teachings and lectures had a huge impact, bringing theosophical ideas to a large audience.

The influence of theosophy took another direction in 1912 when theosophist Rudolph Steiner left to form a new spiritual movement called anthroposophy. Central to its creed was the law of reincarnation, whereby the individual soul learns lessons from one incarnation to another. Steiner developed a new holistic view of education, based around notions of reincarnation and the development of the child. He saw art, literature, dance and music as having a vital role to play in children's spiritual development. Privately funded Waldorf Schools were set up in many parts of Britain to teach the Steiner method of education which aimed to develop a unity of mind, body and spirit, long before the term became fashionable.

The most extraordinary mystic movement that took root in inter-war Britain was Mazdaznan. Its eastern guru was Dr Otoman Zar-Adusht Ha'nish who travelled around the country addressing packed public meetings. He had revived an ancient Persian religion which advocated a system of special breathing, diet, exercise and prayer to achieve self development and spiritual purity. The exercises were based on yoga and included singing and humming. The motto of the movement was 'breath of life'. Abstention from meat and alcohol were essential for devotees. The movement particularly flourished in northern towns and cities like Halifax, Huddersfield, Ilkley, Keighley and Leeds. Dr Ha'nish died in 1936 but even a year later there were still fifty two Mazdaznan centres in Britain.

Dr Ha'nish: controlled breathing and meditation were the paths to self-fulfilment.

A few began to embrace mainstream eastern religions. The British Buddhist Society was formed in 1907 and by the 1920s had established a temple in Chiswick where followers could meditate. The most influential figure in the early development of British Buddhism was Christmas Humphreys, a leading London barrister. His religious search was precipitated by the death of his brother during the First World War. The emphasis he placed on the notion of rebirth in Buddhism was part of a broader interest in the idea of reincarnation after the mass trauma of the war. During the first half of the century, however, Buddhism appealed only to a very small group of a few hundred devotees in this country. It was often a quiet, intellectual pursuit, engaged in by be-suited middle-aged men in the reading rooms of public libraries. Nevertheless, there were a handful who made the pilgrimage east to take the vows of the monk. It involved a life of strict discipline, obedience and hardship that often contrasted dramatically with the material comforts they had enjoyed back home. Men like Robert Albison, a clothing salesman from Rochdale who left for Thailand in 1957, were the pioneers of the hippie trail to the East which became so fashionable from the late sixties onwards. From this moment on, the image of Buddhism changed completely and the spiritual quest for a new consciousness would be forever linked in the public mind with drugs, sex and bohemian youth culture.

Eastern religions appealed so much to rebellious middle-class youth in the sixties because they reflected many of their aspirations and concerns. They embodied a search for individual meaning and personal enlightenment which were very different to the dogmas of the Christian church. At their heart was a mysticism, missing from western religion, which aspired to a transcendental experience similar to that which young people were getting on drugs.

In the late sixties Hinduism also became fashionable amongst the young. One of the first Hindu-inspired religions was the Hare Krishna movement (The International Society for Krishna Consciousness). It was popularised by George Harrison who in 1969 recorded the hit single 'Hare Krishna Mantra' based on the Hare Krishna chant. Sanyassin devotees, many of whom were ex-hippies, shaved their heads and wore saffron robes. They believed that it was possible to achieve spiritual enlightenment by constantly chanting the name of God. By the seventies there were a host of similar eastern-inspired religions flourishing in Britain which attracted the allegiance of tens of thousands of young people. Amongst the most influential were Elan Vital or the Divine Light Mission, Osho International with its guru Bhagwan Shree Rajneesh and Nichiren Shoshu, a recently revived offshoot of Buddhism. Most have survived the death of their leaders, internal divisions and recurrent newspaper exposés about sex, drugs and cult mind control. At the dawn of the millennium they have become established as part of the modern mystic landscape of Britain.

AILEEN PRESTON

I was a society woman. We were often guests at Viceregal functions when the Viceroy and the Vicereine came to Hyderabad on their first port of call. The women wore long white kid gloves and we were all dressed up. But there was another side to India that I encountered, a spiritual side. In India you had this feeling of the ancient past and how much had been created by spiritually thinking people of many different religions.

I came across semi-miracles all the time. I've seen people walking bare-footed over fire, and they came through unscathed, not feeling any sense of being burnt. We all accepted it as being absolutely as it appeared to be, you just took things like that for granted. I remember once a yogi came to my husband's college to talk and to demonstrate what yogis could do. He was a very remarkable man indeed. He asked my husband to fetch him a bottle of prussic acid from the science laboratory and then this guru poured the prussic acid into the palm of his hand and it turned very black. He got himself into a certain position, evidently moving the organs of his body, and then he swallowed it. And I and other people thought, well that's wonderful but when this talk is over he'll disappear into the loo and he'll vomit, but he didn't. He stayed much longer and obviously there was never any question of getting rid of it. The power that the mind and spirit can have over the body is amazing. That wasn't even the spiritual aspect of what yogis can do, but I was fascinated by it all the same. You can't live in India for some time without these things having an effect on you.

Aileen is as old as the century. She was born in January 1900, the daughter of a sea captain, her mother a suffragette. In the early 1930s she went out to India to join her husband, a teacher in Hyderabad and enjoyed the life of a memsahib. She soon discovered the mystical magic of India and her own gift of spiritual healing. She returned to Britain at the end of the Raj and developed her skills alongside the renowned healer Harry Edwards. During the 1950s she ran a healing service from her home in Romford. She came across yoga and meditation while living in India and still practises them today at the age of 99. She lives in Hereford and has one son.

When we first went out to India, my mother was suffering very badly from fibrositis. We took her to one of the doctors there and he gave her the usual drugs to ease the pain, but like me she was very much against taking more drugs than you absolutely need. So we were at a dinner party one night sitting next to a very hard-headed businessman and told him her trouble and he mentioned a woman called Frances Murray who had cured him of something serious. We made an appointment to see her and she gave my mother the laying on of hands and healing and after three visits my mother had lost every symptom of pain and was fine.

But this Frances Murray really astounded me by saying, 'Well, Aileen, I am looking at your hands and I see them greatly enlarged and surrounded with light, which means that you are a natural healer.' I objected, I was pleased with what she'd done for my mother, but I was fond of pleasure, parties and acting and I couldn't possibly imagine myself ever becoming a healer. She said, 'Well, time will show, Aileen, but I can only tell you that you've got hands that were intended to heal.'

Soon after that my head boy came to me one day complaining of a bad headache and I said, 'Well, Murray Memsahib tells me that I have healing hands, I might be able to help you, would you like me to try?' 'Oh, please Memsahib,' he replied and off came his turban. I spent about ten minutes with him and he said, 'Oh Memsahib, all pain gone. All better. Thank you.'

Well, after that, all my servants would come to me with their various complaints and they also brought their wives and children and in almost every case there was a complete healing but I still didn't believe in it fully. Until one day they brought a man, laid him down on the verandah, he'd been bitten by an extra large scorpion and had this tremendous swelling on his shoulder. He was in agony. So I said, 'Oh, poor man, I'll get the car out and take him immediately to the hospital.' 'No, Memsahib, Memsahib will

Aileen was the reluctant healer of her Indian servants.

do.' I said, 'This man is in agony, I've been able to help all of you with your small things but this is not a small thing and Memsahib can't possibly do anything.' 'Oh yes, Memsahib, you can do it,' they said. And in the end they won and I said, 'Well, you all come in, you're a Muslim, you're a Hindu, you're a Parsee and so on. Let us all pray to our own God that this man be healed.' I worked on him for about half a hour and he said, 'Pain now here, now here,' and we continued until he said, 'Oh, Memsahib, pain all gone now, oh.' So from then on I did a great deal of healing work among Indians and Europeans.

'In those days, we kept quiet about being spiritual healers.'

I would take a person's hands and help them to relax the whole body and the mind and then I would put my hands on that part of the body that needed healing, then work down the spine. People would feel strong vibration and sometimes great heat. In fact, I knew one man who said, 'For heaven's sake stop, Aileen. I can't bear this heat.' It was so strong.

I felt that to the true Indian mind, healing and a deeper understanding of perhaps you might say the other world, of things not of everyday, was on the whole very easy for them to accept. People would talk about the knowledge they had gained from previous incarnations. I know I've had many hundreds of incarnations. I have one very clear memory of being in Ancient Egypt and I was some sort of slave. I have glimpses of concocting herbal medicines for sick people, so maybe I was a healer in a previous life.

We returned to England eventually and heard of a weekly healing session where the person who gave healing would go into a deep trance and while in trance could tell the patient exactly what was wrong and recommend certain very simple remedies. I had hearing restored to a deaf ear which I'd had since childhood. And we hadn't been going there very long before this trance healer who called himself Golden Feather said to me, 'What are you doing here little Memsahib, you should be working.' And I said, 'What do you mean, Golden Feather.' 'You know very well what I mean, you have been a healer and you've got to do it again. Next week you're not coming here to have healing, you come to work.' And that was the beginning of my work in England. I put on my white coat and once a week I held a healing session in my home. One little girl came to me. She was just four years old and had been given a year to live by the specialists. Her parents believed in spiritual healing and brought her each week and each week there was progress. At the end of the year she was absolutely perfect and they took her back to the specialist and he said, 'there's no need to bring her again, there's nothing to worry about'.

My husband and I kept quiet about the fact that we were healers. We just felt that we were mixing with a lot of people who wouldn't understand and perhaps wouldn't approve. It's surprising the number of people who have in due course come round to accepting these things. I don't think that people would say that you were an oddbod now if you told them that you were a spiritual healer, but they did then.

EILEEN DE CRESPO

Theosophy affected my development. Before it I was a normal English girl with average desires and wishes to get on in life. But theosophy made me more alert, a freethinker. I became so interested in wider questions. I heard that there was a theosophical college in Letchworth, Herts called St.Christopher's. There I started being a little different, going to that college and meeting other theosophists. The curriculum included nursery school training with Maria Montessori. She was a very elegant lady and one of the first women doctors in Italy. She knew that the first stage of the learning processes is through your senses so she invented apparatus for the children to play with that helps them discover things for themselves. One of the tools was an alphabet embedded in sandpaper so that the children could feel the texture of the lettering.

One of the threads of theosophy was that every few thousand years there is a teacher, a superman comes to the Earth to teach humanity. Buddha was one, Christ was another. The leaders of theos-

Eileen was born in 1906 and brought up in Bristol. As a child her mother took her to lectures at the Theosophical Society whose magazine was called *The New Age*. There she came across ideas such as the brotherhood of man. She trained as a Montessori nursery teacher under the pioneering Maria Montessori at St.Christopher's, the theosophical college in Letchworth, Herts. It was here that she met her Spanish husband Ricardo. They went to live in Spain but after Ricardo was imprisoned during the Civil War they escaped back to Britain. Eileen was an early feminist. She knew the Pankhurst family and during the 1920s was a flapper who led marches for the emancipation of women in Bristol. She later became one of the first female accountants. She is a Buddhist and has been blessed by the Dalai Lama.

ophy in India observed a couple of boys and came to the conviction that one of them was suitable to become the new World Teacher. Krishnamurti was brought back to Britain and bit by bit he was trained to be the next World Teacher. Part of the teaching of theosophy is that we have got to the stage where we have produced supermen, some of whom have physical bodies. Three of them were the inspiration for the Theosophical Society. They were the Masters and they lived in the

Theosophist Eileen de Crespo (left) as a child selling flowers to raise funds.

Himalayas. The story goes that one of them trained Krishnamurti every night when he was asleep and when he woke he wrote down everything that he had learnt in a book called *At the Foot of the Master*. So he was well trained to be the World Teacher.

They set up an organisation for him called 'The Star in the East'. Every year, for the young people who were interested in hearing him, there was a camp at a castle in Ommen in Holland. I went with a group of young theosophists to see him at the Friends Meeting House in Euston Road in London. I'd heard so much about him, I thought he must be a wonderful person. He was a handsome man. I had the impression of being in the presence of a beautiful person.

India was very significant. I became involved in India because of theosophy. One of the leaders, Annie Besant, was a pioneer in getting the Indians to start working for their own freedom. She was involved in the India League working for Indian independence and I took part in that. We organised meetings and lectures about India and tried to get people interested. I met Gandhi when he came to London. He was a little man dressed in Indian clothes sitting cross-legged on a mat. He was very impressive. I wanted him to come to Bristol to talk, but he was unable to make it.

To be a theosophist, an active theosophist, you had to take part in all the big problems and questions that were going on around you in society and

Eileen de Crespo, aged 93, pictured in her Bristol flat. 'We thought we were the harbingers of a New Age.'

of course, at that time, one of the problems was votes for women. There were three classes that did not have the vote: aliens, criminals and women. I felt very strongly about that. The suffragette movement had gone through a hard time. They had to do extraordinary things to show men that they should give the vote to women, but then the war came along. Mrs Pankhurst, the head of the women's movement, turned it into a helpful organisation and she was willing to suggest that women helped in the factories. When the war was over in 1918, they had to give the vote to women, but women were not to have the vote until they were 30 years old. The men had it at 21. So that was a time when I became more active in it and it was called 'votes for flappers'. We held marches and meetings to get the vote at the same age as men which didn't happen for another ten years, and then it became universal suffrage. I don't know if aliens and criminals were included, but women did certainly get the vote then!

I was asked to stand in the municipal elections as a Labour candidate in Bristol West, then a very conservative area. The big programme was to introduce public ownership in all walks of life. It all came from the Industrial Revolution when the workers had been terribly exploited. I don't know why I was so active, maybe it came from my previous incarnations.

I became convinced that it was cruel to slaughter animals just to eat them. It really disgusted me. I remember going to the coal mine in Pucklechurch to see blind ponies and being outraged by the treatment of these animals. We tried to organise a party of young people to go to an abattoir to see the reality of slaughter but we weren't allowed in. It just reached the point one day when I said no, I wouldn't eat any more meat. So I became a vegetarian. They thought you were very peculiar being one and it was quite difficult, but it was a link up with Eastern religions and ideas to dispense with killing animals.

For the young theosophists in the 1920s it was a time of great hope and great joy too, and of great activity. We all believed that the world would be a better place for all that we were doing. We thought there would indeed be brotherhood throughout the world and that there would be peace between the nations. We were very optimistic, we thought we were the harbingers of a New Age.

GRACE GOODMAN

In India, I was brought up by lots of servants. I used to love their stories of their gods and it never struck me that people didn't believe in reincarnation. It was a belief that I grew up with. A couple of my aunts were spiritualists and they had spirits that did table rapping and would answer their calls. Now my aunts had a theory that you must never lie, so I never doubted them. So all these supernatural things were natural to me.

It was when I was a young wife in Manchester in the thirties that I first heard of Krishnamurti. I went to see him speak and there was an aura about him that permeated the room. He was young, he spoke with fervour and he spoke with belief, his eyes were shining, he was wonderful. Spontaneously people stopped talking and it was like electricity. He was electric. Wherever I looked everybody's eyes were fixed on him. We'd never been to meetings like that, for one man to hold so many hundreds of people spellbound, there was no sound, it was unbelievable. He was to us a world teacher, the new Messiah. We felt he was the teacher who was going to lead the world into the New Age. The New Age he was bringing in to me meant freedom, equality; women were going to be more equal, there was going to be peace, it felt like a privilege to be alive at that time.

Krishnamurti had opened a door and shown me a way, but the New Age didn't happen. I was very disappointed. I didn't go and see him for some time and my ordinary life took over again. I had a baby daughter, Rachel. She was the apple of my eye, she was my dream come true. Then the war began. I was friends with one or two other Jewish mothers and we were very fearful of what would happen. We heard terrifying stories from the refugees of the horrible things that the Nazis did to Jewish children, that they would amputate

Grace was born in Calcutta in India in 1910 where her father was a property dealer. She had two brothers and one sister. She first came to England when she was sent to boarding school at the age of eleven. After leaving school she settled in England and became a secretary when she was nineteen. She married her husband, a salesman, in 1934. Their only daughter, Rachel, was born in 1938. At the beginning of the war Grace was alarmed by stories of Nazi atrocities on Jewish women and children. Fearing for their own families because they were Jewish, Grace and her friends devised a method of committing suicide rather than suffering in the event of an invasion. In 1957 Grace was inspired by the guru Krishnamurti's message of unconditional love to set up an experimental community in Surrey to house some of Britain's most deprived and violent families. *The Big Issue* made her 'Londoner of the Year' in 1994 for her work with the disadvantaged.

*'If you've got
        the flame, you're
part of humanity.'*

their arms and legs to see if they could live. I couldn't bear to think of my daughter's lovely chubby limbs being hurt or torn and we were filled with fear. We were terrified at what would happen when the Nazis invaded and came to Manchester.

So I got together with my women friends and we agreed on a suicide pact if the Nazis invaded. I knew a Jewish doctor and he gave us some cyanide pills. Our plan was that when we heard the church bells, which meant the Nazis had landed, we would have a party with all our children. We had stored away some of our food, some sweets, some chocolates, everything that the children liked, and we would give them all the nicest things. Then at the end we would get them to eat the pills to kill them. When we were sure they were dead we would take the pills ourselves. I would have done it because I loved Rachel, I didn't want her to suffer. I knew reincarnation was a fact, I knew it was true and that we would meet again in the after-life, we would be together. That was what would have given me the strength to do it, but thank goodness I didn't have to.

When the war was over, I began to get involved again in a kind of New Age thinking but at the time nobody saw it that way, they just thought it was a bit of madness. Krishnamurti had started me on the road. He taught me to care. He said that if you are never cared for by others you can't care for yourself. It was around 1957 that I began to get interested in parents who couldn't cope and where the children were taken away from them. I'd got friendly with these sorts of women in Manchester and I liked them, they were often warm, loving and friendly. I thought it was wrong to break them up, why couldn't they be kept together? I wanted to do something about it. I wanted to do something for the families that Social Services couldn't do anything with, the real problem families. At the time, people thought I was mad, it was absolutely revolutionary.

Anyway, I was on one of my trips to India where I had seen a swami and he told me my prayers would be answered and I would be trained. On the boat coming back I met Mrs. Gainsford who was coming to do some social work in England. We got talking and she shared my ideals, so we decided to start this project together. Our total capital was £1,500 from each family and we bought a large country house at Frimhurst, it had thirty six rooms in all, in twelve acres. It was ideal. And there we started our dream, which was to give these families a place where they were cared for, loved and respected. We got the most hopeless families about to be broken up with children due for adoption and we were allowed by the authorities to try to do something with them.

Well, we started Frimhurst but I had no idea how to run it to achieve our ideals, because I had no training except in ordinary social work. Then I was walking in the woods and I saw this golden figure with wings and looking at this figure I knew how Frimhurst was to be run. We were to live with the families. And the principles would be freedom, love and acceptance of who these

people were. They wanted to swear so I let them. Some of them would come up to me and say, 'piss off Mrs. Goodman'. They said that helped them so I agreed with that. The most important thing was that they could say what they felt, to get it off their chests. I found that the families blossomed, we really did something with them to bring them together.

But one day I was attacked by one of the dads. There was a dispute and he hit me in the face, then when I was on the floor he decided to use his feet as well. I was in intensive care for some time; every bone in my face was smashed. My sinuses were smashed, I have none now. My nose was smashed and my jaws were beaten. I have steel plates in my jaws and I still suffer from lack of feeling on the left hand side of my face. But I recovered and I came back, I was determined not to give in. We carried on in the same way, with the same freedoms, but I introduced a no hitting rule and the families eventually agreed to this. The man got two years in prison, I remember I went to see him and he said he did it because I reminded him of his mother. He said he would have swung for his mother, he hated her, but she died when he was eight.

One of the things that came to me after this experience was that I saw a little flame in everybody around their chest, some clouded, some clearly. It was this that helped me get into relationships with a lot of families that would normally put me off. I said, 'if you've got the flame, then you're part of humanity.'

DAVID CLEMENT

David was born in 1911 in Staines and grew up in London and South Wales. Both his father and grandfather were Clerk of Ascot racecourse. While at school David came across the Eastern ideas of reincarnation and karma in books by the philosopher and one-time theosophist Rudolf Steiner. David was so enthused by Steiner that he dropped out of Pembroke College, Oxford to join the pioneering community of Sunfield near Stourbridge, an alternative therapeutic home for handicapped children which used revolutionary methods. He married the principal's daughter and had three sons and one daughter. David still lives close to Sunfield.

At school my brother and I were fascinated by Ancient Egypt and Atlantis and we always looked for books about them. We found a copy of *Atlantis and Lemuria* by Rudolf Steiner in Foyle's bookshop and this fascinated us both. We then went to a lecture at the Rudolf Steiner Hall in 1928 and it was wonderful. I went everywhere saying to people, 'You know it's possible to know where you've come from, why we're here on Earth, where we're going to.' I couldn't understand why no one seemed very interested.

We bothered the poor masters at school with all this. I came back from the holidays one year and said to the history master, 'Oh Sir, I've heard the most wonderful thing, that Gladstone was the reincarnation of Cicero, isn't that amazing?' And he threw back his head, roared with laughter and said, 'Clement, who am I the reincarnation of?' ' I don't know sir,' I said. 'I, my boy, was an abbot,' he said and I thought, by George, I believe perhaps you're right. Anyhow they were very kind to us even though they must have thought we were completely crazy with these ideas. My brother and I both felt that we'd lived before, that we'd been in Ancient Egypt. Steiner developed the ideas of reincarnation and destiny and how they work in the human life and in life after life after life.

Later my brother was drafted out to India and before he'd been there six months he had died of typhoid. But in his last letter to me he wrote about how he wanted to go and work at Sunfield, a Steiner community for curative education which helped handicapped children. Well, I felt I must go to Sunfield so I left Oxford where I was a student. The Dean of the college told me I couldn't leave until I was twenty one, but I said, 'Well, on the day I'm twenty one I'll go there even if I've got no money. I'll walk, but I'm going.' In the end he relented and said there was no point in my coming back and I left at Christmas 1931.

Sunfield was one of the first children's homes in England run along Steiner lines. The whole approach to the children was through the arts. There

were twenty or thirty of us including artists and musicians and I found the place extraordinarily alive. We made our life entirely around the children. We slept in the nurseries with them. We ate with them and played with them. There was one adult to one child. The whole life of the children was centred around preparing for the next festival and we used to work with them through plays.

One child was very frightened to take a step up from the floor and so the whole play was built around helping him to take that step. So many things were done to help the child get another stage further. And we rejoiced when somebody did the simplest thing they couldn't do before. It was like a family really because we were all in it together, children and staff, and birthdays of course were great occasions. We had very little money for personal possessions.

It wasn't until after the war that these children were recognised as real human beings. Before the war it had been a terrible stigma on any woman to have a backward child and she wanted nobody to know about it. In one case we had a child who was terribly deprived. When he was born the matron at the hospital had said to his mother, 'what have you done to have a child like this?' and the poor mother committed suicide. This was the most dreadful experience. The attitude to handicapped children then was not to waste your time on them, they couldn't ever be normal. But at Sunfield it was said that if you do nothing with the child, if it just lives and feeds and washes then, when it dies, it has nothing to prepare for its next life. Whereas with these children even if we taught them the smallest thing, that would help them to incarnate whole in a future life. That thought was quite inspiring.

'The attitude to handicapped children was not to waste your time on them.'

'It was the spiritual dimension that fascinated me.'

It was the spiritual dimension that fascinated me. You could see that why a person is backward may not be as a result of his or her immediately previous life – it may have been the life before or even the life before that. Steiner showed us that if you lead a very immoral life and do bad things you will be very handicapped in your next life, but when you meet a handicapped child, that wasn't always the cause. It might be a noble soul who wishes to experience life in a deprived state and then they go through this life as an experience to make them all the richer for a future life. When we were working with children we often had a fair idea which it was, which child was a noble soul and which child had done terrible things in the past.

We had quite modest aims, such as helping a child so that it could stand still and then could move harmoniously without jerks. Then Steiner brought the art of eurhythmy into the world. It was movement to music and to speech, and these therapeutic movements were used to help the children. The movement affected them completely. You tried to bring their soul into harmony, told them stories to make them cry, to elate them, to invigorate them and bring life to them.

BORIS PUKATSCH

Boris was born in 1908 into an Orthodox Jewish family, the fourth of five children, and brought up in Leeds. His father was a craftsman making slippers by hand and his mother came over from Russia as a child. After school Boris became a tailor, eventually joining the family business. He first saw Dr Ha'nish, the Mazdaznan guru in 1931 and became a Mazdaznan himself the following year, adopting the exercises, diet and meditation that went with it. During the war he was conscripted into the civil police force. On retirement in his early seventies, Boris embarked on an Open University course and was awarded a Bachelor of Arts in Humanities at the age of 80. He lives in Leeds with his younger sister Rita.

I first saw Dr Ha'nish at Leeds Town Hall in 1931 when I went along with a group of young friends. It was a good job I got there early because otherwise I wouldn't have managed to get a seat. He made his entrance in long robes and had an entourage of musicians on the platform, they introduced him and sang a few songs. It seemed like there were at least a thousand people there listening to Dr Ha'nish and they were even standing in the aisles. There wasn't much public entertainment then, so any speaker who came to Leeds was sure to get a good audience, but this was something more.

He spoke about all sorts of things. We took part in the songs, the exercises and great stress was placed on breathing and glandular exercises

in particular. I realised then that this was the path and I had no difficulty in embracing the Mazdaznan philosophy. It appealed to those people who wanted to improve their physical and mental state. Breathing and meditation were the key, and alongside that you had to live a life free from vices. The idea behind breathing was that 'exhalation ends all strife, inhalation means inspiration.' We concentrated on the essence of breath which if done consciously would stimulate the brain. At the Sunday services we would do a three-minute breathing exercise. You'd concentrate your sight on a spot card, sit with your spine erect and breathe in for seven seconds and then out for seven seconds. We found that three minutes of breathing was enough to relax us and rid our lungs of carbonaceous substances.

Dr Ha'nish was a master. He was the greatest man I ever knew of. He seemed to know everything and had met all the great thinkers and teachers of the late nineteenth century. The masters of the day in the East thought that the West might not be ready for a master, knowing the way people lived then, but he came to teach health, all kinds of knowledge, agriculture, science and philosophy. He could look at your head, the phrenology, and know whether you were spiritually inclined, physically inclined or intellectually inclined according to the shape of your forehead.

At the beginning of every meeting there was what we called a divine philosophy and one of the first exercises we would do was to sing and use the electricity of the fingertips over the magnetism of the heart to become conscious of the heart which is where the ego entity is. So we would vibrate our fingers over the region of the heart and sing, 'Have in your heart sunshine and all is well.' We were encouraged to do it two or three times a day.

Dr Ha'nish was one of the first to know about endocrine glands. We were taught to do exercises to stimulate the glands. The thymus gland supposedly

The young Boris Pukatsch and friends embraced the Mazdaznan way of life.

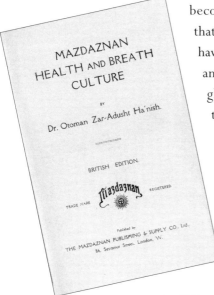

becomes dead at puberty but the Mazdaznan philosophy says that as long as you can keep the thymus gland activated you'll have a happy disposition. So we would vibrate over the glands and sing, 'Stir, stir the glands, stir, stir the glands, stir the glands and make demands upon the minds to meet all ends, tra la la la la la la la la la la.' The tra la la was supposed to activate the pituitary gland.

The leaders would dress up in light-coloured robes. Dark clothes were considered part of the adverse nature and I was encouraged to wear light, and as I was a tailor at the time, that was no problem. I always wore white trousers. You were there to represent the brightness and lightness of life, the light on Earth, that was part of the philosophy.

During the war I was a conscript police officer in Leeds. I still found time to do my breathing exercises and daily meditation, to live cleanly and wholly. I would do my beat on a bicycle with a lamp strapped to my waist shining downwards in case there was any chance of bombing, those were the conditions that we had to deal with. We'd hear the noise when there were enemy planes going over and British fighter pilots would go up and engage them in battle. Some people were scared, of course, and sitting in the air raid shelters I would do the breathing exercises to stay calm until the all-clear sounded. Because of that I never got agitated or started screaming.

Dressed in white, Mazdaznans attend a meeting in Southport in the 1930s.

ROBERT ALBISON

As I was growing up I felt that there was a void in my life, I was always looking for something that would help to explain the void, something that would be fulfilling. I tried all the normal things, like the Christian approach, but I wasn't very impressed at all. Neighbours of ours were Catholics and one of the daughters, my girlfriend at the time, invited me to go along to a Catholic church. It was very theatrical, people were very devout and the priest came along and scattered his holy water and so on. It was all very impressive, but as we came out of church there was a sort of stall where they were selling icons, crucifixes and figures of the Virgin. The priest was there blessing these icons with a cigarette hanging from the side of his mouth and smelling quite strongly of Scotch and I didn't think it was quite appropriate so I turned my back on Catholicism from that moment. The next disappointment was deciding to go to the local parish church one Sunday. I asked some friends of mine to go along to back me up in this. Unfortunately we arrived a few minutes late. We were allowed in quietly and directed to sit at a pew quite near the door, heads turned and we were given looks as much to say, 'what are these three scruffy kids doing here?' It was a brief brush but it was enough to put me off and I suppose that's what caused me to look elsewhere.

As far as I could see, the Christian church had become meaningless. It dealt in symbols, it was a charade almost, just trying to please but not really meaning anything to anyone, not the congregation, not even those who were participating in it. For me it seemed to be fundamentally missing the point, asking people to be faithful without answering questions. This was a far cry from the Buddhist point of view.

Born in Rochdale in 1932, neither Bob nor any of his family anticipated that at the age of 25 he would be a Buddhist monk. Bob left school at 14 and like most of his friends stayed on in his home town and found a job as a shop assistant. When he discovered Buddhism his life altered dramatically and he left Rochdale for Thailand, a country he had hardly heard of, let alone imagined visiting. After returning from Thailand Bob had a difficult time readjusting to life in Britain but after some years met and married Doris, and moved to Nottingham where he started a career as a cabinet maker. They still live happily in Nottingham with the only traces of Bob's former life being the odd statue or image of Buddha hidden between their collection of Victorian and Edwardian antiques.

I first came across Buddhism when I read something called *The Sacred Books of the East*. Buddhism seemed to have the answers, the more I read the more convinced I became. Here was a doctrine that was better at explaining the situation: one's feeling about life, what we're doing here, what we are about. All these things you can test for yourself, if it doesn't fit the situation then you can reject it: there are no 'thou shall nots' in Buddhism. You can undertake to restrain from a certain course of action but you do not have to, that's a positive approach. All the answers were there for you to see for yourself, you didn't have to take anything on faith, and I think that was the inspiration that kept me going on the path of Buddhism.

It was a personal thing to begin with and I didn't talk to many people. I just read as much as I could lay my hands on. Eventually I found out that there was a Buddhist society in London and so I wrote to them and was invited to become a member. Through this I discovered that there was a society in Manchester and Manchester was quite easy for me to get to, so I joined the group there and used to go to public meetings.

Robert Albison:
'there are no
"thou shall nots"
in Buddhism.'

It was in Manchester that I came across the man who gave me the idea of going to Thailand. He had been ordained as a bhikku, a Buddhist monk, in Thailand and had returned to the UK to assemble three or four men who would go back to Thailand, be ordained as monks and then start a Sangha, a kind of 'order of monks', over here in England. When I heard about this I jumped at the opportunity, I thought it was a great chance to be able to advance myself spiritually.

My family were quite supportive of my decision. My father wasn't very happy but he had left us when I was eleven years old. I had very little contact with him and so didn't even ask him what he thought about it. My mother just said, 'So long as you're happy I don't care.' So off I went with a clear conscience.

I first had to go to London where I was ordained as a samanera, a novice monk. During the ordination I had to approach the bhikku as a lay person, all dressed in white and with my head already shaved. Someone lent me a pair of white cricket trousers for the occasion.

I asked permission of the bhikkus to be ordained and to 'go forth'. They gave their permission and I was handed the robes. I went to a side room and put them on, then approached the bhikkus again and did obeisance to them and asked again to go forth. They welcomed me into their order and gave me a new name. I exchanged my name Robert for the name Sudawardor which means 'he who spreads confidence'. I was happy with this name as I thought it might inspire others to follow in my direction. After ordination I felt elated, it gave me a new lease of life. I'd left all the luggage behind me, this was a new personality, a new me if you like, it was a feeling of relief. The past was past. Now I had a new life, a new going forward, going forth.

We had arranged to go to Thailand before the ordination and by this time there were three others who had also taken the robe, so we were a group of four. It was the first time I had been abroad and to find myself on an aircraft in robes amongst dozens of other people was quite an experience. The reception when we got there was extraordinary. We arrived at Bangkok in the dark and you could see the silhouettes against the terminal building of hundreds of bhikkus, the monks, all lined up to greet us. It seemed incredible that so many people were interested in Europeans going there.

Our routine at the Wat, the temple, was entirely different from anything I had experienced at home. You got up at dawn, which would be four, four thirty in the morning. There would be a short period for meditation and then you would ideally go 'pintaparta' which is to go begging for your food. It wasn't strictly necessary but, idealists that we were, we preferred to do it. It was the way that Buddha laid down, that food should be begged for and so I was quite happy to do it. It is also laid down how one should beg. You have to maintain your concentration by casting your eyes on the ground three paces ahead of you. When you were aware that someone was waiting there to offer you food you approached that person, held out the bowl and food was put into it. This is the way you continued until the bowl was full. Sometimes you would be given rice, sometimes little parcels of food wrapped in palm leaves with skewers in, sometimes a piece of fruit or a whole fruit was put into the bowl. You waited until you returned to the Wat to

MAN WITH A NEW NAME, NEW LIFE

MOTHER SEES TAILOR SON TURN MONK

Express Staff Reporter

BOB ALBISON, 24-year-old tailor from Rochdale—Gracie Fields's home town —was renamed last night Saddhavaddho, when he became a Buddhist novice monk.

Barefoot, wearing yellow robes that left his right shoulder bare too, Robert Albison knelt and bowed his shaven head six times to the floor in front of three Buddha statues.

His mother—a cleaner for a Rochdale engineering firm—was among the congregation in the Buddhist temple in a house in Ovington Gardens, Knightsbridge.

She handed him his yellow robes—the first of the clothing that will wear down now on—as part of the ceremony.

Then he repeated the ten rules of moderation before joining monks. Three were from Ceylon, the fourth from Burma. The purpose, the yellow-robed Bob Albison Kaukhvadho, is, 'He who spreads confidence in the world and his means within himself increase.'

He heard Chief Bikkhu the Venerable Gunasiri say, 'I renounce the world, I find the wicked life, its worldly pains.'

CHANTING

The ceremony lasted an hour. The sandalled monks moved silently into the room at nine o'clock came—the time for daily devotions and the prayers Buddha. He led them in ...

Then Albi...

BUDDHIST NOVICE ALBISON
You're not to sleep on a high bed.

'A monk's life was not easy for a European.'

look in the bowl and eat. It could be anything: fish, meat, chicken or just vegetables and, of course, rice.

Life as a monk was hard, the climate was difficult, the mosquitoes were difficult and for a European it's not an easy life. It's all right if you're staying in an air-conditioned hotel but when you are staying in a hut, with just a mosquito net for protection, it's pretty hard going. We also had no money and no control over money, we had to rely on lay people for our money. We had nothing other than the things we were supposed to have as a monk, which were very few. You had your three robes, your begging bowl, a pair of sandals, a needle and thread to repair any tears, but that was all you could call your own. Everything else you had was communal. If you wanted to go anywhere it had to be arranged, if you even wanted to send a letter to the UK you needed help. We had no money, no stamp; someone else had to provide it.

You felt some obligation to these people who were putting themselves out for you and providing for you. But slowly I began to realise that what they wanted contradicted what I felt was right. I was a novelty as a Westerner. I was being asked to go up and down the country to participate in different ceremonies, because in this way they could draw big crowds of people and drawing big crowds meant making money. The press and film crews followed us around the country and I certainly hadn't anticipated that life as a monk would be like this.

Gradually, I did become disillusioned. I felt that perhaps I had made a mistake. At first I was unwilling to admit that things weren't quite right and I hoped that if I hung around then maybe all this razzamatazz would die away and I could carry on more peacefully meditating and studying. But eventually I decided that I'd had enough. With hindsight I think if I'd given it time things could have worked better for me, but I was young, I was inexperienced and I was naïve.

Coming back to England was traumatic, even more traumatic than leaving, because by this time I had nothing. I hadn't even any clothes to stand up in. I had no money, no resources. I'd no one I could turn to, to borrow money really. It was difficult, much more difficult than the step of taking ordination in the first place. But one finds a way.

RANCHOR PRIME

I had a very religious background. I was a choirboy at Westminster Cathedral and then went on to be educated by monks at a school down in Sussex. Religion was always part of my life but in those last few years of my teens I was busy getting away from it, as far away as I could. I was an art student at Chelsea Art College on the King's Road, so I was quite at the hub of things, that was in 1969. I was experiencing the freedom of being out there in society, an art student, and I found I very quickly lost faith in the materialistic sort of life. I was looking for something deep, something spiritual and of course in common with all my friends of that generation we experimented with drugs, LSD and so on. Although I know that there's a negative side to that, one of the things that it did for us was it really opened our minds, it sort of expanded our awareness.

Born in Leeds in 1950 Ranchor moved to London as an art student at the height of the sixties hippie scene. It was while he was there that he came across the Hare Krishna movement and made the decision to leave behind his bohemian lifestyle. He joined the first Krishna temple in London and became a devotee in 1970. Ranchor lived in the temple until 1987 during which time he married and had two children. Although no longer living in the temple he is still a devotee and works for the International Consultancy on Religion, Education and Culture. He lives in London with his family and is a journalist.

I'd actually reached a stage where I'd finished with all of that and wanted to find something more permanent and safer, something more substantial, that's when I met the devotees. I think at that time, the East held a tremendous appeal to young people, the 'Mystic East'. It provided a tremendous spiritual tradition but one which was different to the West. My first contact with the Krishna was through the musical *Hair*. It had arrived in London sometime in 1970 and one of the centrepieces of the musical was the whole cast dancing on stage and singing 'Hare Krishna'. My sister bought the record and it really caught my imagination, I used to sing 'Hare Krishna' without really knowing what it was about. Around the same time the Hare Krishna devotees had arrived in London and recorded a track with the Beatles. Everyone then started singing it. I was one of those people, I heard it on the radio, I began to sing it and that was really, in a subtle way, what actually got me involved in Krishna, just singing the name of Krishna, not really knowing what it meant but feeling the power of that mantra. It sort of entered my subconscious at that time.

The next connection I made was when I saw Prabhupada being inter-

'Please shave my head. I want to give it all up, I just want to be here and have no more distractions.'

viewed on a BBC2 talk programme. Here was this seventy-year old Indian guru, talking about God and basically saying the practice he taught was simply to chant the name of God, that's all, nothing else. I thought I must have missed something but then he offered to demonstrate and just walked across the studio, to where a group of his disciples were sitting and he sat down, too, on the studio floor. Now in that kind of programme I'd never seen anyone sit on the floor, they always sat on armchairs. Then they started this divine sound and began singing the Hare Krishna chant. 'Hare Krishna, Hare Krishna, Krishna, Krishna, Hare, Hare,' like that, repeating it over and over again and slowly the programme faded out. I turned to my father, who was also watching the programme and I said to him, 'Wasn't that incredible, wasn't it divine?' and he said to me, 'I didn't see anything special about it.' I was really shocked, because it moved me to tears but hadn't touched him at all. That was a very important moment for me, because that's when I made the connection between what I had just watched on tv and the chanting, which I'd heard on the radio – before I hadn't really understood that it had this very profound background.

After that a number of things just sort of happened in my life by serendipity. I was in the public library, not really knowing what I wanted to read and I came across *The Bhagavad-gita* translated by Christopher Isherwood. It is the sort of essential sacred text of Hinduism. On a whim, I took it out and sat down and read it for hours and hours. I was enchanted by it. At around this time I used to help a friend run a stall on Portobello market every Saturday. The devotees from the Temple also started going there every Saturday to sing. They would come down through the crowds in a row, a double row, men and women, about ten of them usually, swaying and singing. It was almost as though they were floating down, there was incense, they had joss sticks burning and there'd be this wonderful sort of apparition drifting through the crowds, chanting. And so in that way I began to see them.

Within a matter of weeks a friend of mine said to me, 'You know, I've been going to the Krishna temple, you'd like it Richard, you should come down.' So I went with him and visited the temple. As soon as I got there I had this feeling, I immediately knew that I belonged there.

I decided I was going to live with these people and there was a terrible hullabaloo. Everyone thought it was a terrible idea. My family didn't take it that seriously, to tell you the truth. 'Ah, we'll give you a month, maybe two, and you'll move on to something else, we know you.' The principal at Chelsea Art College was appalled and had a long discussion with me, trying to talk me out of it. But I just really felt in my gut this is what I've got to do, no one is going to deter me. The next morning, I got a phone call from my father, who said, 'Richard, I've heard you've moved into the temple, do me a favour, I've spoken to the monks at Worth,' which is the monastery where I went to school, 'Will you go and stay there for a week and discuss it with them, because we're all a bit worried.' I said, 'Sure, it sounds like a nice idea.' So I stayed with the Benedictine monks for a week, during which time I spoke to everyone in the community about how wonderful Krishna was. I think at the end of the week they were actually quite pleased to get rid of me.

At the end of the week, I went back to London and I moved into the temple on that very same day. I said to one devotee, who'd become my friend, 'Please shave my head, I want to give it all up, I just want to be here and have no more distractions.' He got out the razor and shaved my head and it was a wonderful feeling, I had quite long hair actually, being a hippie. I then remember saying to him that at last I now felt surrendered to Krishna. He said, 'You don't understand, to surrender to Krishna is a much, much deeper thing than this, it'll take you a long time.' I understood this in future years, that it's a constant act of surrender, that's what the spiritual

'I was looking for something deep, something spiritual.'

part is, moment by moment trying to recollect that I am a servant of God, but that was the first significant step for me, shaving my head.

We had this system in the temple that somebody could live there for six months to make up their mind whether this really was for them or not and then, after this time, could go through the process of initiation or ordination into the life. I took the vows after six months; the vows are no intoxication, no gambling, no sex outside marriage, and a strict vegetarian diet. I took these vows, plus the vow to chant on the prayer beads a certain number of times every day. At that point I received my spiritual name, my Christian name is Richard. I received the name Ranchor, which is a name for Krishna, it means one who leaves the field of material activities and goes to the spiritual, so my name is Ranchor Das, which means servant of Krishna.

For me, taking the vows and living the life of a celibate monk wasn't difficult, I never actually thought about the life I had as an art student and didn't miss it at all. When I arrived at the temple, I just felt I'd come home. Everything about it: the smell of the incense, the figures of Krishna and

Young devotees like Ranchor took the message onto the streets of London.

Rada in the shrine, the way the devotees dressed, the way they spoke, the wonderful vegetarian food; all of this just came together into a total experience and I felt at home, it was almost like falling in love, I just knew there was no going back from this.

The experience of living in a Hare Krishna community could be quite extreme in the sense that it is a very serious commitment and dedication was asked of everyone. Each day was very structured and there was a sort of monastic routine. We had to get up at about half past three in the morning and have cold showers. There was then an early morning period of meditation, using prayer beads and quietly chanting to oneself the Hare Krishna mantra, over and over again. This is a profound prayer, so it focuses the mind. The idea is that the name of Krishna is a sound incarnation of God – he's present in that sound so if I chant the name of Krishna, it's as if God is dancing on my tongue. In that way we used to spend hours chanting and then studying the scriptures, so every morning, the first four or five hours of the day, would be spent in spiritual practice, either chanting, praying together or studying the scriptures and listening to talks on the scriptures.

Another part of our daily routine was to go out chanting. We used to go out morning and afternoon in groups of four or five or six or ten, chanting, singing the Hare Krishna chant with a drum and cymbals. Every morning we would go to Oxford Street and then in the afternoons we'd go to Hampstead, or the King's Road or Kensington High Street, all the places where people were. I'm actually a very shy person but it felt so right I didn't feel shy at all, I felt this is what I'm meant to be doing with my life and the whole idea of the chanting is that the sound of the mantra is enough.

When we were chanting on the street people would stop still and just stare; they'd get their cameras out, point, some people would laugh, some people would shout rude things, that was all part of the experience. I've had rotten eggs thrown at me and tomatoes but perhaps most disturbing of all were the police. Often as not they would just arrest us and in fact it became a kind of game of cat-and-mouse in the early years. Somebody would spot a policeman coming and we would run off down a side street and there'd be a ridiculous sort of chase going on. Mostly we ended up being arrested and appearing in court for obstructing the pavement.

After a while, in Central London, people got used to us but at weekends we would go to the provinces where we sometimes had extraordinary experiences. I remember going up to Manchester to open a small Krishna centre. The first time we went on the streets in Manchester, to the main shopping street, Market Street, such a large crowd gathered that the traffic couldn't get past and the whole street was blocked. Then all of a sudden there were police sirens, vans swooped and took us off to the police

Beatle George Harrison popularised the Hare Krishna movement with a hit single.

station. We were arrested and the next day we were in all the newspapers in Manchester – 'The Hare Krishna people have arrived' – it caused a tremendous sensation.

In one sense, for us, it was like a game – we were all very young and we enjoyed it, we had a good time, it was exciting. In another sense we felt very seriously about what we were doing, we felt that we were like brave new warriors representing this spiritual revolution that we felt must take place in society. Everything seemed so materialistic at that time. I suppose our youth made us very idealistic and we felt we were doing something important so it didn't matter if the police arrested us, if we had nothing to eat, we just somehow had to go out there and confront people. We weren't interested in getting into debates about philosophy and so on, we just wanted to confront them with this idea of dedication to God.

In Hindu tradition, as in many other religions, there is an ideal of celibacy. Those few who can remain celibate and totally dedicate themselves to God are regarded with great respect. In Hinduism there is also the idea that there may come a time in one's life when one feels, 'OK, I've engaged with the material world, I've had a certain amount of happiness and satisfaction through my senses and through the places that life has to offer, but now I'm going to move on, I'm going to leave that and devote myself fully to the spiritual path.' I think I, and many of my generation, tried to do it the other way round. We tried total dedication in our twenties and later discovered that we weren't ready for that yet.

I got married in 1979 and after my son was born I remained in the Temple as an administrator. When my second child was born, my daughter, I began to retreat from full involvement with the community. I found that bringing up children involves a whole different set of attitudes towards life, I was looking more to see how one can live in the world as a Krishna devotee. That's really my main focus now – not to separate oneself from the world and live in a sort of airtight community, but to incorporate the principles of Krishna consciousness, which is to love and serve God, into one's daily life. Many of my generation of Krishna devotees are trying to do the same. But having had that taste, having experienced that purity and single-mindedness of a celibate, dedicated existence, it is something that remains to haunt me – always there in the back of my mind as something to which I want eventually to return.

BEWITCHED

I N the 1950s lurid and sensational reports appeared in the popular press claiming that witchcraft was still alive in Britain. Almost every week Sunday newspapers ran reports of Satanic abuse, wild orgies in the woods and desecration of graves. However, most of those who practised witchcraft had no interest in the black arts. They followed instead the wiccan tradition of 'white' healing magic. It was part of an extraordinary revival of paganism in Britain which saw the parallel growth of Druidry. Many of those involved in witchcraft were women, often with feminist ideals, attracted by nature worship and the pagan concept of the Goddess. By the mid-sixties there were more than a hundred covens in Britain. Secretaries, factory workers and office managers by day would meet outdoors by night to celebrate ancient customs like the Winter Solstice and the Spring Equinox.

Witchcraft dates back to the very earliest times in Britain. Stone Age cave paintings depicted the Horned Lord of the Animals and represented pregnant women as the Goddess or Mother Earth who brings fertility to all. In pre-Christian societies the use of magic was accessible to ordinary people who would make offerings to invoke helpful spirits. Such rituals reinforced a belief in the supernatural world and sought some control over nature to avert uncer-

ABOVE
In the seventeenth century, the witch was a folk devil. By the 1970s, there were more witches in Britain than ever before.

OPPOSITE
Patricia Crowther, high priestess of the Sheffield coven. In the post-war years, there was an extraordinary revival of paganism in which witchcraft became very popular.

41

tain seasons, disease and natural disaster. Sorcery could be used for good or evil ends, to assure fertility in the fields or to punish enemies. The roots of wicca were greatly influenced by the Celts: the four major festivals of witchcraft including Hallowe'en, the festival of death, were derived from Celtic celebrations. Witchcraft was also influenced by the centuries-old country tradition of 'wise women' and 'cunning men' who used their knowledge of herbs, cures and spells to act as healers and midwives solving the problems of villagers.

From the late 1950s onwards, the tabloids orchestrated a modern day witch hunt.

Christianity condemned witchcraft, claiming that all magic and miracles not clearly from God were the work of the Devil and therefore manifestations of evil. In fact, witches never worshipped the Devil which is a Christian concept that postdates pagan beliefs. Witch-hunting reached its peak in the seventeenth century and by the end of the eighteenth century between 40,000 and 50,000 people had been executed as witches in Europe. In 1736 witchcraft ceased to be a capital offence in Britain but remained illegal. At the turn of this century it was still common practice in parts of rural Britain for elderly women to be accused of witchcraft and blamed for local blights such as failed crops and sickly animals. However, in 1951, the belief was that the Craft of the Wise no longer existed and the old Witchcraft Act was finally repealed.

There is some evidence that witchcraft in Britain did survive into the twentieth century through the traditions of a few families like that of Paddy Slade, a hereditary witch, whose forbears were consulted on health matters and affairs of the heart. In the 1920s Cecil Williamson, who opened the Witchcraft Museum on the Isle of Man, embarked on a personal search to find the remaining witches in Britain and found nearly a hundred scattered about the country.

The witchcraft revival in the late twentieth century is largely due to the efforts of a retired civil servant named Gerald Gardner, who is widely linked with rescuing and reinventing witchcraft in modern Britain. Gardner, an English customs officer posted to Malaya, believed himself to be the descendant of a witch called Grissell Gairdner, who was burned at the stake at Newburgh in 1610. On retirement, Gardner settled in the New Forest, an area associated with occult activity. In 1939 he came across the last remains of an old-time witch coven and was delighted to join them. In wicca Gardner found what he was looking for – a Goddess-oriented religion which preserved the remnants of traditional village witchcraft and which he believed could offer a spiritual path of the Old Religion to future generations.

With witchcraft still illegal, Gardner was urged to keep the rituals secret but after the repeal of the act in 1951 he was able to publish *Witchcraft Today*, the first account of modern-day wicca. His recreation of witchcraft borrowed from a number of sources including folklore, magic and Masonic rituals and had a major sexual element; Gardner had an interest in flagellation and was also a naturist. Numerous covens sprang up under Gardner's guidance, first in Britain, then Europe and North America, many of which still flourish today.

The revival of witchcraft during the 1950s attracted much attention from the press. Most of this was moral panic underpinned by a deep fear of the new sexual freedoms of the time. White magic was always far more important than black magic in the pagan revival. The new recruits to the covens included those who wanted to worship the ancient faith of a Goddess as well as a God, those who came from traditional witch families and people who had had psychic and mystical experiences. They met at night in natural settings to worship the Nature Gods and performed rites by firelight and to the sound of drumming and chanting to build up power with which to cast spells. Much of the magic performed was with a view to helping those in the coven with their personal problems and others who sought their advice. The magic involved drew on the energy of Nature and the psychic abilities of those in the coven. Sex was viewed as a powerful positive force that could be channelled into spells. Members might take a partner within the coven to produce sex magic. Although witchcraft was now legal, most people kept their nocturnal pagan activities secret for fear of losing their jobs, homes and families.

The huge growth of neo-pagan witchcraft in the 1960s and '70s was spurred on by the sexual liberation of the time. Most converts were middle-class women in the creative arts, academia and the professions. The emphasis on the Goddess, Mother Earth, and the reverence for the reproductive cycle were all seen as empowering for women and brought wicca into the realm of the women's movement. Today, witchcraft is at the centre of pagan beliefs and paganism in turn is one of the West's fastest growing religions.

Gerald Gardner, the retired civil servant, who rescued and reinvented witchcraft during the 1940s and 50s.

PADDY SLADE

I am a hereditary witch, I'm not traditional or modern. Most of what I've learnt is from my own family from a very long time ago. We go back a very, very long way. We were lucky enough not to be wiped out although there were quite a few of us who were burned at the stake. I had read a lot of fairy stories as a child in which the witches were always portrayed as being evil and doing a lot of harm, but I remember what my grandmother was like and what my parents were like – they weren't evil and what they did was good, they helped people.

My sister used to take me to see my grandmother when I was little. She was a very old lady and had a tiny little cottage and a tiny little herb garden. My sister wasn't at all interested in what was happening, but I used to go holding Granny's hand round the herb garden and she would tell me that this was for that and you used this for something else and if someone had a stomach ache you would give them that. I always thought it was a fascinating thing, even as a very small child. I felt from the time I was about four or five that I would probably follow the path my grandmother followed and if they called my grandmother a witch, then they would call me a witch too.

She had a very well stocked herb garden which was unusual in the nineteen thirties. Herbs are usually quite nondescript, they don't have flashy flowers, and they have little leaves as a rule so you don't waste space in a small garden on herbs, unless you're doing it for a specific reason. My

Witchcraft runs in Paddy Slade's family. Both her parents and grandparents were witches. She was born near Canterbury in 1931. She thinks of herself as a 'village wise woman' and usually works alone. During the early 1950s she served in the WAAF in Singapore where she met her husband and traded herbal remedies with Malay witch doctors. She took up the craft full time in the 1960s when she was living on Dartmoor. The widow of a Signals Sergeant Major, she has passed her gifts onto her sons. She lives in the countryside west of Bath, in the last house in her village – coincidentally, the house traditionally reserved for the wise woman.

grandmother had a very specific reason, because people would come to her with pains and aches and sprains and breaks even, and she would say, 'well, we will do this for you, we will give you that,' and my mother was the same. There were all sorts of things like using couch grass for digestive ailments and the tops of nettles make probably the best blood purifier there is. Even bindweed, which was called devil's guts, is good for the bladder and that's an absolutely hellish thing to have in your garden.

You must remember that in the thirties people had to actually pay to go to the doctors, they had to be on a doctor's panel in order to get treated. They had to pay for their medicines and usually the witch could do it cheaper and give them more time. My grandmother used to have women come to her whose husbands were aggressive both sexually and physically. She had a little potion which was guaranteed to calm down any rampant male and she passed it onto me – my mother knew it as well – and it works very well indeed.

Later, during the war, all the witches got together to perform an important task. Round about the early part of September 1940 it was becoming obvious that England was going to be invaded if the German Luftwaffe could get supremacy over the RAF and the witches, all the way round the coast, wanted to make sure that this didn't happen. My brother was in charge of some of the cross-Channel guns and officially you couldn't get down to the beach because it was mined. But my brother knew how the mines were sown and a couple of days before this invasion was supposed to happen, he, my mother and grandmother and various other old grannies – there were about a dozen of them – all went down to the beach right on the tip of Kent. As the tide turned so that it was ebbing, they

45

'I have a very close relationship with a spirit I call Puck.'

AN APPLE LOVE SPELL

Pick your apple when the moon has waned three days. Breathe upon its green cheek, rub it with a scarlet cloth and say:

Fire sweet and fire red
Warm the heart
and turn the head

Kiss the red half, put it in another's hand. Who holds it shall weaken; who eats it shall be yours.

threw what we call Go Away Powder into the tide with such invocations as 'You Can't Come, Go Away, Bugger Off' over and over again. And the invasion never happened.

Go Away Powder is a very ancient recipe and it will get rid of almost anything. I know that people might say this is rubbish, sheer imagination, but the powder has this ability to push stuff away from you. You can do it in your own house if you've got things that you don't want like mice or starlings, but push it into an ebb tide which is going to take it out, then it will work much better because of the salt in the sea.

In 1942 I was living in Canterbury with my family. The town had been blitzed as a reprisal raid for the terrible raid on Cologne and people went and slept in the woods because the Germans had dropped high explosive bombs on the water mains. We went out into the beech wood and slept in a tent and one particular night I was having a dream, in fact I've never been sure if I was asleep or awake, but I got up and I went out into the woods. I arrived at a stream with all the flowers and plants that you would normally see throughout the year, all there. There were also many animals around this stream, there were badgers and foxes and stoats and all the animals that you might see in a wood if you were lucky. But on the other side of the stream from where I was sitting there appeared this great, big creature. He had a magnificent spread of antlers and I looked at him and said, 'Are we going to die?' And he said, 'No, you're not going to die, you've got a lot of things to do before you die. You've got a lot to learn.'

He started telling me some of the things I would need to know, some of the things I was going to learn, and then at one point he said, 'I'm going to take you to meet somebody,' and he put me up on his horse and we flew — up through the trees to a very beautiful place that was quite a long way away. I met the Goddess for the first time and she told me what I would be doing with the rest of my life. She said that I would probably forget most of it until the time was right for me to remember it and then she disappeared. I returned to my tent and in the morning told my mother all about it. Because she was a witch, she didn't say, 'Rubbish, child. Stop imagining things.' Instead she said, 'Now what you have to remember is that you have to grow up in the world, do your homework, but you must never forget.' So I didn't tell anyone about it, I was a loner anyway, and gradually it came back. I have since met the Horned God, the Goddess and I have a very close relationship with a spirit that I call Puck, the old one of the land. It's through my contact with them I've been able to become a proper witch.

I was in the WAAF during the fifties. They had this phrase 'Roman Catholics and Jews may fall out' and then the padre would come and he'd take a service. He'd do prayers and give a little homily and you listened while you were standing at ease. Well, one day I got rather fed up with this because I'd heard it all before and I didn't believe a word, so when they said Roman Catholics and Jews may fall out, I fell out too. There was a roar from the adjutant who said, 'What the hell do you think you're doing woman, come back on parade.' I said, 'I'm a witch, sir,' and he shouted across the parade ground, 'What do you mean you're a witch?' I said, 'I'm a witch and I don't believe in Christianity at all, it's not something I have any feeling for. Roman Catholics and Jews have fallen out, so I've fallen out too.' And so I stood there for the rest of the parade, and afterwards I was marched in to the adjutant, who started tearing me off various strips and eventually gave me three days' jankers because I'd been insubordinate.

My husband died in 1963, so I took my children to live on Dartmoor in a very, very isolated village, with no telephone. I started to go back to all the things that I'd learned. The thing that started me off was a woman giving me a pot of chives and I started thinking, 'I remember about herbs, this is something I can do' and I started making myself my first herb garden. I became known as someone who could cure various things. It was a long way into the town and the doctor didn't like coming out very much and so when you have someone who has an ability to do some healing, people are apt to come and knock on your door. The first time I was approached was by a man who lived at the other end of the village. His wife was quite ill and she couldn't sleep at all. I made her a little herb pillow and a potion of various herbs which she took and she started to sleep. He paid me by keeping me supplied with fresh vegetables all the year. There was also a woman who lived next door and was absolutely overrun by earwigs. So I made up a powder that got rid of the problem and in return she used to look after my dog.

TO PROTECT THE HOUSEHOLD

Take five hairs from a golden broom bush. Using them as tapers, carry them throughout the house asking good fortune to come as you say:

> *Wraiths of the House,*
> *take heart and fire.*

> *To every chamber light I give*
> *To every corner this breath I send*

> *Help this house in which I live.*

For added efficacy, sprinkle the floors with a mixture of orris root, tea leaves and salt, then sweep them absolutely clean.

Spells from Natural Magic, A Seasonal Guide, *Paddy Slade, publ. Hamlyn.*

Cecil Williamson

I spent the summers with my uncle the Rev William Russell Fox, vicar of North Bovey. One afternoon I had in my mind to toddle off after lunch and scrunch some of Uncle's nice dessert gooseberries, so to the kitchen garden I went. But I quickly realised that there was something going on over the high stone wall in the central green of North Bovey. Dogs were barking, children were squeaking and there was a general hum of conversation, so I dropped the idea of gooseberries and went to the garden gate. Sure enough there was something going on – there was a whole gathering of people, so being an inquisitive little so and so, I hopped across the road and made for the centre of things. I arrived just as four burly agricultural types were stripping the last garments, down to complete nudity, of a little old lady who lived quite close to the vicarage. She was absolutely stark naked. I don't know what drove me, there was some impulse, but I pushed my way forward and threw my arms around this naked body lying on the ground and hung on like grim death. I was kicked, I was beaten, I was punched, but I hung on and on and, all of a sudden, everything went dead quiet and a pair of more friendly hands came down and lifted me up. There was Uncle, saying 'Cecil, go back to the vicarage at once.'

Cecil was born in 1909 in Devon. He came from a well-to-do military family, his father was in the RAF. When he was a boy, he went to the rescue of a witch being tormented by village labourers. This first encounter sparked off a lifelong interest in witches and their supernatural powers. Later on, Cecil embarked on a tour of Britain in search of the last remaining witches. During the Second World War he set up the Witchcraft Research Centre and was asked by MI6 to monitor any dangers presented by Nazi occultists and astrologers. After the war Cecil opened a witchcraft museum in Windsor which had a resident witch called Rosa Woodman, but he was asked to close it down when members of the Royal household suggested that it wasn't suitable for a public witch to be on the doorstep of a royal residence. Cecil took the hint and relocated the museum first to Oxfordshire and subsequently to the Isle of Man and then Cornwall. A widower, Cecil now lives in his beloved Devon where he spends his days sorting through his collection of witches' remains and magical tools.

Later my uncle told me what had happened. The men had been having trouble with their pigs – dying and that sort of thing – and when you have trouble people look around and find a reason for it, and in those days, they thought it could be witchcraft – particularly in the remoter parts of the county and they'd had a run in with this little old lady called Mary. So they blamed her and they'd come down into the village and been in the pub all morning and were shouting out in the street and letting everyone know that they were going to prove to the people of North Bovey that Mary was a genuine witch, an evil person. So they dragged her out of the house and onto the green and they had a bit of a harangue and then they started to strip her off. They did this because they were going to prove that on her genitals she had the third nipple or teat of the devil, which was a sure sign of witchcraft.

A couple of weeks later I was going down to the village to post some letters and as I was passing Mary's little cottage I heard a squeaky voice say, 'You be the young mister as tried to help me the other day.' She invited me in, we talked about this and that and, from that moment, there was a growing rapport, although it was mostly above my head. I was only six years old but it did open up a whole new world to me.

Cecil Williamson helped MI6 in the war against Nazi occultists.

As I grew older, I was moved to a more upmarket prep school at Norfolk House, Beaconsfield, and there one used to get beaten up badly by the prefects. They were pretty beastly and there was this wretched fellow by the name of Bulstrode, a big brute of a fellow. Well, on this particular evening I'd been beaten up and my half crown postal order was taken away from me. I'd resisted and I'd got a black eye and a cut cheek and was in a pretty poor state. Well, I went down to the kitchen and there was a visitor wearing a nice coat and she said, 'Good gracious me, little fellow, what on earth's happened to you?' Anyway we sat down and were having a chat and mention was made of North Bovey. Cook butted in and said, 'Oh you've got a lot in common because this lady you're talking to is a sort of witch or wise woman.' So I unburdened my heart about Bulstrode and this woman said, 'Would you like me to

Cecil in old age, reflecting on a life devoted to the study of witchcraft.

help you? I said, 'How?' And she asked me what I would really like. I said I'd like for Bulstrode to not be here because he's a pain in the neck to me. So anyway it was arranged between cook and this good lady that I should go up to her house.

One day I wandered up the road to her rather nice cottage and she introduced me to the witch's swing. To make this, you find a tree with a suitable bough and get some rope and make a swing. But there's one extra thing, and that is to make yourself a little bonfire and put lots of grass on it so that it reduces the flame and produces a column of smoke. So you sit on the swing and as you swing backwards and forwards through this rising column of smoke you use a mantra. A mantra is whatever your wish is. In my particular case I said, 'Take through the smoke, Bulstrode away. Take Bulstrode away.' You go on doing that for not less than about twenty minutes.

After the holidays, the time came for us to go back to school. The usual thing at the beginning of term is to look at the lists and find out which dormitory you're going to be sleeping in. Everybody was milling around doing this and I kept on looking but I couldn't see Bulstrode's name anywhere. So I plucked up the courage and said to the matron, 'excuse me, but I haven't seen Bulstrode.' She pulled herself up. 'Haven't you heard, he won't be coming back.' Well, how can I explain the emotions that went through me at that moment, it was as if you'd thrown a bucket of cold water over me, it couldn't have been greater. Anyway, I made enquiries and what had happened to Bulstrode was that – great big snotty fellow that he was – he'd gone skiing to Switzerland and like everything else he was a big know-all. He'd gone off piste and made the mistake of trying to go round both sides of a very stout Swiss fir tree at once. What he'd done to his crutch and pelvis is no-one's business, but the long and short of it was that he was in a wheelchair and was liable to be like that for the foreseeable future. The emotional effect that had upon me as a young boy was terrific. I had to face the fact that there I'd been deliberately going to some trouble to put a curse on him and it had worked.

From that time I took a great interest in witchcraft, curses and spells and wherever I went into the countryside I used to ask around if there was a village witch or wise woman. I found that there were quite a number of women in the villages who were able to help people who brought their problems to them. Some dealt with medical problems and were midwives, others with the problems women were having with their husbands. If the client who'd come to the witch wanted a person removed, the witch would go to the trouble of making up a doll with a decent head of hair and very often they would do what I call humming magic, they would hum and rock – and they'd work to the theme and chant 'Go, go, go, go' and 'Away, away, away, away' or 'Leave alone, leave

Cecil opened a number of witchcraft museums after the war which attracted local opposition.

The Enquiring Eye of

THE WITCHCRAFT RESEARCH CENTRE

Brings to you an explanation and understanding of the practice of witchcraft both past and present day.

LEARN How the Witches make their spells, potions and medicines.

SEE The articles used in witchcraft ritual.

STUDY The arts of divination together with hundreds of other amazing and interesting exhibits connected with the practice of witchcraft.

WHEN IN WINDSOR BE SURE TO VISIT

The WITCHCRAFT EXHIBITION
The HIGH STREET, WINDSOR
opposite THE GUILDHALL

Open every day, Sunday included
From 10 a.m. to 6.30 p.m.
ADMISSION 1/-

The Exhibition is presented by
THE WITCHCRAFT RESEARCH CENTRE

alone, go back to your home, go back to your home' and that went on and on. If the witch couldn't help, she'd say, 'Well, I'm afraid dear that I can't help you, but so 'n' so in the next village, she's absolutely excellent on that sort of thing.' Times are different now as places like Boots the Chemists have come in, so a whole lot of things that you would go to a witch for, now you'd go to Boots.

In 1938 I was approached from out of the blue by a Colonel Maltby from MI6 who knew my father. He'd heard about my interest in the occult and he wanted to know if I could get him a list of names of leading Nazis in Germany who were dabbling in the occult. So I called myself the Witchcraft Research Centre, and with my notepaper and visiting cards I went over to Germany and met people who were interested in 'this nonsense', as Maltby put it. I was able to give him a list of over two thousand top ranking officials. In Germany, they were still suffering from the First World War and there was a terrific upsurge in interest in what the future held for them as everyone was concerned about their jobs.

When the war started I was sent for by Colonel Maltby and found myself working for MI6 at Wavendon Towers, near Bletchley, where I was commissioned to run a little radio station broadcasting propaganda to U boats. It was like Radio Luxembourg. I got hold of American jazz music which was the 'in' thing then and had a German lady as my assistant by the name of Rita Zimmermann, who had the most sexy voice you could ever wish. The object of this operation? There was a German submarine out in the Atlantic busy sinking ships, but it had to come up every night in the darkness to clear the boat, the hull with fresh air and also to recharge its batteries and let the crews have a cigarette on deck. My idea was to give them a happy hour where they could listen to all this jazz music and to make them homesick. We would use the occult because everyone in Germany had heard of Nostradamus and so we would work in this little thing about 'Oh, by the way you remember what Nostradamus had to say about the sea?' Well, the one thing about Nostradamus was that he was making predictions which were always warnings about not to do this and the other thing.

As it turned out, we were quite successful because the German High Command, we found out after the war, did complain that the U boats were coming home sooner than necessary when they could have stayed out a few days longer.

DOREEN VALIENTE

My favourite pastime as a child was to terrorise the neighbourhood by riding round and round the streets on a broomstick. I was fascinated by the idea of witchcraft. One side of the family came from the New Forest and the other from Cerne Abbas in Dorset and both of these places had a relationship with witchcraft. I used to listen to stories about Grandfather Peckham and Great Aunt Nance who were supposed to have been on rather good terms with the fairies in the New Forest. Fairies were always reckoned to have had an affinity with witches. When my parents caught me listening to these stories they would change the subject and make remarks about little pitchers having long ears.

Doreen is widely regarded as Britain's most influential high priestess and responsible for shaping much of modern witchcraft. She was born in 1922, her family coming from the magical New Forest, which according to local folklore was inhabited by supernatural beings. Her parents were chapel and would have been horrified to know that their daughter would grow up to become a witch. Doreen was initiated in 1953 and became Gerald Gardner's high priestess before hiving off to form her own coven. During the war she married a freedom fighter from the Spanish Civil War. She lives in Sussex, the last county in England to become Christian.

When I got older I started drawing figures of a horned head, like the old horned god. I never used a pencil or crayon, it was a charred stick.

My mother was a great crossword fan and I used to get hold of her dictionary and look up all the words I could find connected with the occult like talisman, amulet, magic. Why I did that, I don't know, maybe it was harking back to a previous life but things like that would bother my parents.

There was a turning point during my childhood. When I was about nine or ten we were living in a little country place in Surrey. One night I looked out of the window at the moon. There were no street lights and it was the first time that I saw real moonlight, everything was silver. I just stood and watched it, amazed. Not long afterwards I was leaning on the garden gate in the twilight and I had a spiritual experience. I saw, just for a moment, the painted veil called life. Some people can look at the painted veil all their lives, but some people see it shake and I saw it. I saw the world of forces behind the world of form. I had experienced what was beyond the physical and it was wonderful, it wasn't frightening. Later I was searching for something that worked, that opened the door, that really parted the veil. The old pagan gods appealed to me because they were the personification of the forces of nature. They spoke to me far more intimately, in a wood, at night looking at the moon and stars, than anything I had ever come across in church.

I did some early experiments with magic. My mother was working as a housekeeper in a big house. There was a woman working there also called Hilda who was very unpleasant. She set out to make life miserable for my mother and I got so fed up with hearing about it that I said, 'Mother, why don't you let me have a go at this woman?' She asked me what I meant and I replied, 'Well, I've learnt a bit about magic and I think I could curb her activities a little.' So I asked her to fetch me something that belonged to Hilda, some hair or something that she'd worn. My mother laughed but she agreed to do it just for a joke. She sneaked into this woman's bedroom and got some hair out of her hairbrush and I got hold of some beeswax, a nice selection of black-headed pins and a few herbs, and I made a little puppet of this obnoxious woman incorporating the hair in it. I said a few of what I thought were the right words and stuck in a few of the right pins and a very funny thing started to happen.

A large blackbird started following Hilda about the house and pecking on the windows wherever she went. She was terrified. But the trouble was that Mother was terrified, too, because she'd only done it as a joke and was horrified to discover

Now the witches have their own 'trade union'

Brighton witch Miss Doreen Valiente with some of the tools of her "trade."

ITS name is almost staid—the Witchcraft Research Association. Even Magic Circle sounds exotic beside it. But its aim is to delve into the history and practices of a subject which some say is vile. Others mildly amusing. . . .

The association was formed earlier this year and has still to hold its first meeting. But its pre-dictably enough was born on Brighton Crescent on the seafront.

There lives Doreen Valiente, one of Britain's few witches. Self-styled of witch's "muddy and there is no university degree, tidied there with a Witch's diploma and one with a Wart's diploma and one passes nails loosely round and one . . .

She refers to a number of the occult she says, to initiate £1 of association. Our perfectly genuine research into the old tradition of people who have just body of and sincerely and honestly fascinating subject, study a very . . .

A COVEN

The association, she agrees, has yet to meet. But it has been my its aim for all months of existence. Miss Valiente says it is . . .

● Discovered a coven—active witches—before to gro . . .
● Collected a number of . . . associations not before a . . .

THEY FORM A RESEARCH ASSOCIATION

helped in clairvoyance, Miss Valiente is after a sample of that too.

The association has produced one issue of a four-page magazine about witchcraft. It said for it. Another is due shortly.

Miss Valiente is proud of her claim to fame, which she has with plain to make. So far she's pleased with progress of the association, cautious about giving information about people where very said about where there has been so anyone the worst sort of publicity she said.

She estimates that she is one of only a number of witches in this country but as she says, many people have been a about people have been, the old religion which W.R.A. although like to collect not yet attained substance.

it has a great future.

would like to see it open an office in a London library hold meetings, it is travel relics hold think folk, pagan, is interested in any folk, and wants superstitions in any. accurate statements to combat in-craft. For this instance about it made, the this witches, said Miss Valiente, a dance is the effects link that was actually you, and any a witch's power And meeting and what she must be can in old and dancing in the high summer country in a normal

Doreen Valiente standing by the tree stump in the New Forest known as the Naked Man, the meeting place of the New Forest witches.

that it had worked. So she told me to call it off. I said, 'Oh, very well, perhaps we've given Hilda a fright, I'll stop it now.' So I broke up the puppet and did my own banishing ceremony, I didn't really know what I was doing but it came from somewhere inside me and it worked, much to Mother's amazement. Maybe I was just reliving something that I'd started way back in a past incarnation.

I went to a convent school but I was quickly disillusioned and became a confirmed atheist. During the war I was doing office work in London when I had a vivid dream, a precognitive dream of the Germans shelling the South coast on 13th June 1944, which later happened. That made me more aware of dreams and got me interested in the occult.

Like most people I thought witchcraft had died out, but then in 1952 I saw an article in a popular magazine called *Illustrated* about a new witchcraft museum that had opened on the Isle of Man. It was run by Cecil Williamson and the resident witch was Gerald Gardner. I read this with amazement. I realised that witchcraft was still alive, that people were practising the old religion which they did for luck or fertility or just to be in contact with the old gods or what I had felt leaning on that garden gate. Of course, it had actually been illegal up to 1951 and I'm told that the reason they abolished the last of the old witchcraft acts was that it was generally understood that witchcraft was dead so there was no point in keeping it on the statute book.

I was very struck by the article, so I wrote to Gerald and we got acquainted. He was a very impressive person. He had a great shock of white hair, curious tattoos on his arms and I remember he wore an old suit of Harris tweed and a big bronze bracelet with symbols which represented the three degrees of witchcraft. I recognised in him immediately a person who knew about magic and witchcraft and I felt that I had, at last, met someone who was worthy of being called an authority. He was very interested in nature and naturism as a means of empowering people and ridding them of inhibitions.

He wasn't in a hurry to initiate me because there had been a lot of persecution from the newspapers with stories, most of them made up, about black masses, sexual rites and bloody sacrifices on the altar. He lent me a novel which had descriptions of the witch's initiation rites to see if it would shock me. But of course it didn't shock me or horrify me at all – the idea of dancing naked was jolly good fun.

My initiation took place in a large, private house. I was brought into a circle, sworn to secrecy, given the password and then underwent a ritual of purification. I was shown the working tools of a witch and told the legend of the god and goddess. Then I was walked around the circle and presented at the four quarters to the old gods, the god and goddess of magic, the old horned god and the lady of the moon as a newly initiated priestess and witch. Halfway through, we all sat down on the floor and had the ceremony of wine and cakes. The funny thing was that I was wearing a necklace at the time and when I stripped naked to go into the initiation room something told me to keep my necklace on. When it came to it, they went to give me another necklace but then realised I was already wearing one. I said I'd thought I'd keep it on and it turned out that it was the tradition that a witch wore nothing at her initiation except for a necklace. I don't know how I knew that, perhaps I'd done it before in a previous life.

I didn't tell my family that I had become a witch, my mother would have thrown me out. In the fifties, people were able to sling you out onto the streets or sack you if you were doing anything unorthodox. I was working as a shorthand typist at the time and I managed to keep things very quiet. I had to be careful not to leave anything about, not to wear any witchey jewellery or anything like that. I knew of cases where people were fired from their jobs because they were suspected of being associated with witchcraft and there was nothing they could do about it. After my mother died my husband didn't mind so much. He didn't want to join himself, but he understood when

'I was amazed to discover that witchcraft was still alive, that people were practising the old religion.'

THE WITCHES' RUNE

Darksome night and shining moon

East and South and West and North

Harken to the Witches' Rune

Here come I to call ye forth

In the earth and air and sea

By the light of the moon or sun as I will so mote it be

Chant the spell and be it done.

I used to go up to coven meetings with old Gerald and when I used to say things like 'I've been ordained as a High Priestess, it's my duty to go there,' he would say okay and that everyone was entitled to have a hobby.

We used to celebrate the sabbats in secret around a fire, chanting and dancing. Gerald had some fragments of old chants from a coven in the New Forest and I wrote some verses to make it workable and get the rituals going.

Just for the sabbat night, people could do something different and enjoy being Brother Herne or Sister Diana rather than a builder, housewife, truck driver or whatever.

The most magical sabbat for me was Hallowe'en. It was the time when the veil between the worlds grew thin and the dead used to come back and communicate with the living. We would make a special effort to communicate with the spirits of witches who had gone before and invite them to come back. I remember once, at the climax of a ritual, we saw a beautiful blue light appear; there was no explanation for it and after a few minutes it faded away. It must have been a spirit manifestation.

The thing that upset some people about witchcraft was that we worked naked. Gerald was keen on naturism and of course then it was considered to be the very height of depravity, but you see there is a power in nakedness and the power would come forth if people were totally uninhibited, dancing naked around the circle. The dancing around the bonfire was to work up power for magic, what we called the 'cone of power'. After a while we went into a semi trance-like condition. Sometimes, as part of the ritual, someone would do a bit of whipping to keep the dance going or direct the dancers in a particular way. We did it as a stimulant. The irony, of course, was that people thought it was okay to flagellate if it was to punish sin but if you did it because you enjoyed its benefits, then it was regarded as a perversion. I recognised it as a legitimate part of ancient ritual.

There wasn't any sexual contact in the first initiation but it did come in later on if you wanted it but nothing was forced onto you. If you wanted to have a partner in magic, then the sexual bond between you was very important. I took part in sex rites of witchcraft and thoroughly enjoyed them. The only thing was that you had to lie naked on a hard altar which was not at all comfortable. The sex magic was the climax, the magic just flowed out of it. I know from experience that it works. I know the Christian view is that sex is only in the world for procreation, that is bunkum, because there is only a certain short time in each month when a woman can conceive, so what's the rest of the month for? The magical use of sex is very old, it goes back to Tantric teachings; in fact, witchcraft was described as a sort of Western tantra.

Of course, we got some men who'd come along looking for cheap sex and that sort of thing, but we soon weeded those out because they gave themselves away. We got a few people who were spying on us, too. Mostly we got a good mixture of creative types, artists, poets, writers and musicians wanting to join the coven along with other normal intelligent people and, of course, people who were naturally psychic.

One of the attractions of witchcraft to me was the strong role for women. In most ceremonial magic the women just did as they were told, but in witchcraft it was the women who had the power. The full moon was very important for magic and it was called the feminine light with which women instinctively had a relationship because the moon cycle is the same as the feminine cycle. I found it all very empowering: worshipping the goddess as well as the god, the acceptance of nakedness and of sex as a power in itself, especially in those narrow-minded days of the nineteen fifties when people were so inhibited. I wonder if we witches weren't precursors of the women's liberation of the sixties. I think we were. We started something going on the inner plane, which later manifested itself on the outer plane.

OPPOSITE

The witch's cottage in the woods where Gerald Gardiner's coven met. Doreen was Gardiner's high priestess.

BELOW

Britain's most influential high priestess pictured at her home in Brighton. Doreen wrote many of the modern witch's incantations.

FRED LAMOND

I was the little fat boy. When others were playing, often I would go on solitary walks in the countryside around Lake Geneva. And on a full moon night I would really feel at home with nature. The full reflected light has a tremendous effect on the imagination, our bodies are ninety per cent water so the magnetism of the moon must have some effect on us and stimulate the imagination. Those were basically the early intimations of paganism. Nonetheless, until I got into my early twenties I always had this feeling at the back of my mind that there was something that held the world together.

Fred was born in 1931. His parents divorced when he was two years old and he was brought up by an over-protective grandmother who over-fed him. He graduated in economics from Clare College, Cambridge and worked in London at the Economist Intelligence Unit. He became a witch in 1957 when he joined Gerald Gardner's London coven and later became a member of the goddess-worshipping Fellowship of Isis. Fred is a computer consultant and lives in Austria with his second wife Hildegard.

Then quite unexpectedly I had a profound mystical experience when my first fiancée took the initiative in making the relationship physical. She took control, I was too much the repressed Englishman, totally unprepared. This was in the fifties, before the days of the pill. I was terribly afraid of making her pregnant so I restrained myself and I suppose in the process I gave what is now known as a Kundalini experience which is one of the techniques of sexual intercourse without male ejaculation. And when she climaxed I was catapulted into outer space and time. I had the feeling that I was the male of all species and of all times making love to the females of all species and all times and around us there were all these couples sitting in a circle in a Tibetan mandala. All the couples of the past were looking at us and saying, 'well done, join the club.'

Then in my head I heard an almighty powerful woman's voice say, 'All the empires, political systems, ideologies, philosophies, theologies that men have formulated since the dawn of time weigh less on the scales of eternity than a single embrace of two young lovers or a single smile on the face of a new-born baby as it gazes at its mother the first time.' And that's what gave me the feeling that I had encountered a goddess, a divine power. So I started reading up on comparative

'I was the little fat boy. I would go for solitary walks and on full moon nights I felt close to nature.'

religions and the psychology of sex. Eventually, I came across a description of the love goddesses of antiquity and I realised that it was the goddess Aphrodite that I had encountered.

I felt that if this had happened to me it must have happened to other people, so let's find them so that I can worship her in common with others. Then I found a book that said that the witches of the Middle Ages were the survivors of an old goddess-worshipping pagan cult and that set me on the path. I discovered Gerald Gardner's book *Witchcraft Today* and it rang so many bells. He interviewed me and introduced me to his coven. When I told them about my mystical experience there were nods of recognition. I met them socially once a month until one day one of them said that I was ready to be initiated.

Gardner was a loveable old man. He had a fine flock of hair that he liked to comb to make it look as though he was wearing horns. He had a great sense of humour and was a terrific storyteller. He believed implicitly in reincarnation and felt that he had been a witch in a previous life.

The coven was made up of ordinary

Fred Lamond with his first wife, Gillian Elliott.

people of all ages. There was a financier in the City, a retired colonel who'd been in the Indian army, a couple of housewives, an anaesthetist with his nurse, a salesman and a secretary, and there were a number of younger people like myself who were on the same wavelength. We met in a cottage in the grounds of a nudist club in Hertfordshire. Because the club had many ordinary members who were not witches and who were not bound to secrecy, we had to shield ourselves from them and do our rituals within the cottage. But we would take in the atmosphere in the wood before the meeting and at major festivals we had bonfire parties to which we invited friends

Fred with his second wife, Hildegard Balcarek.

and where we might enact some seasonal rituals.

At the first degree initiation, you're welcomed into the family to learn the craft which is essentially spell-casting; at the second degree one has pretty well learnt how to control one's own energies and then between the second and third degree you learn how to direct the energy of a group of people, the coven. I was blindfolded at my initiation, I had to strip off my clothes and then was led into a room lit by candlelight. When the blindfold was removed I found myself surrounded by naked people of both sexes, some young, some old and went through the rite of rebirth with what I felt was my family. I swore an oath of secrecy and then I was presented with some of the magical tools of the craft which represent the four alchemical elements and which are aids for directing energy when casting a spell.

I found that I was rather good at conducting power because it was like a very strong high voltage electric current running through my body and I would start to hyperventilate, and then at the peak you project the cone of power telepathically in the direction of the person you're trying to heal. Sometimes people wanted help with health problems, sometimes it was for phobias or for people who were out of a job and needed employment.

We worked in the nude and there were good reasons for that. It was so that we could exchange energy through all of the pores of our body with the trees and the grass around us, instead of just with our eyes and our heads. Then there's the practical thing that if you are going to run around and raise energy, it's very much easier to do it in the nude and not trip up over robes. Within the coven, when we were dancing round in the nude, of course, we felt desire for the people of the opposite sex and that too helped raise the energy. Earth energy and erotic energy are very strongly linked, you see.

In the fifties men were supposed to be men and women were supposed to be women. So men were macho, making a lot of money or doing hard physical work. The women were supposed to be all feeling: loving a man, loving children, but basically obeying the man in all things, their will-power was suppressed. But the idea in the craft, the idea of cross-gender initiation, was that each sex should learn from the other and get from the other what is missing, so a man learns from the woman who initiates him to be more feeling and accept his feelings and that it isn't unmanly to cry. The women learn from the men to discover their own power, to assert themselves and have a will of their own. Before my initiation I was very tongue-tied when meeting young women. I only knew how to talk on intellectual matters, I didn't know how to talk about my feelings, but afterwards I became much more self-confident and it balanced me, it helped my emotional life.

The thing that witches are always asked for is love spells, to help people fall in love with them. Well, this is contrary to our ethics because we do not cast spells on people without their knowledge, it's a form of psychic rape. But we can do spells on people themselves to make them more loveable.

One of our members was a woman who was quite a merry soul, but she was unhappily married. Her husband had become impotent and so she consoled herself with extra-marital affairs. And one day she said that she'd fallen in love with a young policeman in her village, but she didn't want to break up his marriage. She asked us to cast a spell so that he would notice her and see her occasionally. Well, that was out of the question, but we didn't want to let her down, so we worked on her and asked the goddess to give Jane her deepest wish. Five weeks later she met Bill, fell in love with him, he fell in love with her, she divorced her impotent husband, married Bill, gave up her extra-marital flings and today forty years later they're still happily married.

'A man learns from the woman who initiates him to be more feeling.'

PATRICIA CROWTHER

When I was a child we lived next door to Madame Melba who was a clairvoyant and a palmist and she told my mother that I would be interested in

Patricia is a witch and a high priestess. She was born in 1927 in Sheffield. Her great-grandmother from Brittany was a herbalist and clairvoyant. When Patricia was 30, a hypnotist regressed her back to previous lives including one as an old witch called Polly in the year 1670. She trained as a singer and dancer and it was while playing a summer season on the Isle of Wight that she met her future husband, Arnold Crowther, a stage musician and ventriloquist. He introduced her to Gerald Gardner in 1960 and after several meetings Patricia was initiated by Gardner into witchcraft in the private Magic Room at the top of his house in Castletown on the Isle of Man. She was known by the magical name of Thelima Aphrodite. Her Sheffield coven has been in existence for over thirty years.

magic. I was fascinated by the moon, I loved staring at it. I was the fairy on the moon at one Christmas party and later I was the leading lady in a revue with a tableau entitled 'The Legend of the Moon Goddess'. Then I read *The White Goddess* by Robert Graves and this told me very forcibly that the goddess had been worshipped all over the world in the past. I had been looking for the feminine figure in deity, the father God wasn't interesting to me. I thought there must be a mother figure somewhere and that's where I found it. Later I found that the goddess was indeed worshipped in a religion that was still active and that was witchcraft.

My husband introduced me to Gerald Gardner. He took me over to the Isle of Man and we got on like a house on fire. He was an amazing man, full of knowledge, a marvellous sense of humour and he offered to initiate me into the craft of the wise. I was anxious to learn all about the mysteries, especially of the goddess. The initiation was

GOOD
WISHES
FROM THE
HEAD
WIZARD

CITY'S ONLY WITCH SEEKS PARTNERS

performed in the upper room of the barn of his house, attached to his house in Castletown. It was a wonderful experience and I just thought how could it be that there was all this going on behind the natural world? There was something so marvellous that had always existed behind the mundane of everyday living.

When you're initiated you come into the craft as you were born, without any ties. The initiation is performed without clothes, you are brought through the triangle of the goddess, the birth triangle and you become a child of the goddess. Of course, I was very nervous. I sat there holding my dressing gown tightly around me and Gerald said, 'You'll have to take that off, you know dear. You can't have that on.' Gerald used to say female witches usually wear a necklace and a smile. So I wore the necklace of the goddess which represents the circle of infinity and also I wore the garter and

Patricia Crowther is crowned 'Queen of the Sabbats' by Gerald Gardner.

this, of course, is a very ancient insignia of the craft. As soon as you're in the circle and things are happening, it all seems perfectly reasonable and proper and you forget you haven't got any clothes on. Not all rituals are performed skyclad, as we call nude, quite a lot of them are performed with robes but the three degrees of initiation are certainly performed without clothes. There's no ulterior motive, it's just a beautiful ceremony and that's all there is to it.

I told people, I didn't hide it because I thought it was a wonderful thing to be a member of the craft, but Mother was often stopped by people in the street who would say, 'What's all this, Mrs Dawson. Is it true they really worship the devil?' Mother put them right and said, 'No, we worship the great goddess, it's nothing to do with the devil.'

I passed through the three degrees

and that enabled me to start my own coven if I wished but I left it in the hands of a goddess for another year. Then a reporter from a local paper asked me if I was interested in meeting people with similar beliefs. I said yes and she put in the report: 'Witch seeks recruits for coven.' People came and knocked at the door and we selected one person who was eventually initiated as the first member of the Sheffield coven. I had plenty ask but not many were initiated. They had to prove that they were sincere in wanting to worship the old gods. They came from all walks of life: photographers, doctors – they were very interested – nurses especially, ordinary house-

wives. We had one gentleman from Scotland, a very clever industrialist and he eventually started his own group from which a dozen other groups eventually emerged.

We celebrated the eight festivals of the year, we had meetings for meditation, we had meetings when we worked magic and we also had meetings to celebrate successful magical enterprises. Sometimes the coven would meet in the open air, we chose a stone circle in Derbyshire. We had the temple in my house and Mummy decorated it with stone wallpaper; it had wooden

'Witches were pioneers of women's liberation.'

beams so it was very atmospheric. We would go skyclad, open the circle and consecrate it with water, purify it with incense, bless the people in the circle and ask the goddess and god to look over and protect us.

We performed a lot of magical workings for other people, mostly to heal them. People used to write hundreds of letters asking for our help even though some of them didn't believe in witchcraft. It was very good to be skyclad when you're working magic because the power comes from the body. You have to raise your nerve power and this is usually done through a circular dance where you go round and round in order to produce a cone of power. You concentrate on the part of the person that needs healing and chant a few words of rhyme like 'Betty must be healed. Betty must be healed.' In the first ten years we think we had 80% success rates.

The newspapers had the wrong idea about witches and what they got up to in the sixties. There was a lot of rubbish written about sacrificing babies and worshipping the devil. There was also this idea that we sacrificed

virgins. I always said that it was very difficult to find a virgin in those days. I was very anxious to tell them how wonderful a religion it is and how we did a lot of good for people. There were some who joined for sensational reasons, because they thought they could take advantage of the rituals being performed naked, but they were swiftly given the boot if they ever happened to be initiated.

I felt I had a mission in those days to tell people about the goddess because for centuries they were used to worshipping a male god. My life changed when I realised that the female is equally important as, if not more important than, the male of the species. The witches were pioneers, really, of women's liberation because, for anything to happen on the physical plane, you have to acknowledge it first on a spiritual level and of course the goddess was being acknowledged by that time on the spiritual level. So women began to assert their position in life.

Patricia Crowther's coven met in her Sheffield home. 'We would go skyclad [ie naked], open the circle, purify it with incense and ask the goddess and god to protect us.'

SPIRIT IN
THE SKY

CHAPTER THREE

DURING the last years of the Second World War there was a spate of prosecutions of spiritualist mediums under the ancient Witchcraft Acts in Britain. They were arrested after plain-clothes policemen infiltrated their meetings and seances. What triggered this state intervention was the extraordinary influence of wartime spiritualist mediums who claimed to be able to contact the spirits of dead servicemen. Their supernatural powers so appealed to a nation at war that by 1944 the newspaper *Psychic News* claimed there were around 1,000 spiritualist churches and one million spiritualists in Britain.

Spiritualism had arrived from the United States in the 1850s, inspired by the supposed supernatural powers of the young Fox sisters of Hydersville, New York, to contact the spirits of the dead. These children attracted immense publicity for their stories of occult tappings in their home. By late Victorian times there was a craze for seances in which rappings, moving objects and disembodied voices seemed to prove it was possible to

OPPOSITE
Medium Colin Evans levitating at Wartley Hall, Finsbury Park, London, 1937.

communicate with those who had died or 'passed over'. In this new movement of spiritualism the medium played a vital role, often providing messages for the recently bereaved from relatives 'on the other side'. The mediums, many of whom were women, frequently used a native Indian spirit guide to pass on these messages.

Spiritualism developed into an alternative religion which stressed the brotherhood of man and claimed to provide proof of the after-life. The strong non-Christian side of the movement was organised by the Spiritualist National Union which was especially influential in northern industrial towns and cities where there was a growing disenchantment with the established church. Keighley, in Yorkshire, was the cradle of British spiritualism where several spiritual newspapers like the *Yorkshire Spiritual Telegraph* and the *British Spiritual Telegraph* were based. In particular it appealed to free-thinkers and autodidacts wanting to explore the supernatural. There were close links too with the early socialist and co-operative movements. Weekly

Psychic postcards from the 1920s. There was a vogue for capturing photographic images of relatives who had 'passed over'.

meetings were often held above Co-op shops and stores.

But spiritualism remained a fringe religion dogged by fraud and scandal. Mediums were under constant pressure to perform. And with seances often held in darkness, sometimes with the medium in a curtained-off cabinet, there were considerable opportunities for deception. One of the most celebrated examples was the appearance of ectoplasm during seances and meetings. This opaque substance was produced by some mediums when under trance. However, investigators revealed a number of cases in which ectoplasm was in fact muslin, chewed up paper or egg white. On the other hand, the Society for Psychical Research, set up in 1882 to research into supernatural phenomenon, recorded numerous cases for which they could offer no rational explanation.

Spiritualism broadened its appeal and was taken more seriously during the First World War in which almost one million British servicemen died. Many families who had been suddenly bereaved found that spiritualism offered comfort and consolation that the established church could not provide. The spirits of dear departed sons and fathers lived on, it was claimed, and could be contacted through mediums.

In the inter-war years spiritualism benefitted from the conversion of a number of influential figures to its cause. One of the most famous converts was Sir Arthur Conan Doyle, creator of the super-rational sleuth Sherlock Holmes. He first became interested in spiritualism in 1917 and became a tireless propagandist for the cause until his death in 1930. Robert Blatchford, the famous socialist writer, previously an agnostic, also became a propagandist for spiritualism. In 1925 the agnostic Hannen Swaffer, at the time the

well known editor of *The People* announced his conversion. He had attended many seances during an investigation into spiritualism and became convinced that he had received messages from his former boss, newspaper tycoon Lord Northcliffe. By

Apparitions like these convinced Sir Arthur Conan Doyle, a tireless propagandist for the spiritualist cause – but they were widely dismissed as fakes.

the 1930s there were more than 2,000 spiritualist societies across Britain, most concentrated in the industrial north, with a total membership of around a quarter of a million.

Spiritualism enjoyed its finest hour however during the Second World War. This was despite the fact that throughout 1939 spiritualist mediums, apparently using their psychic powers, had confidently predicted that there would be no world war. In August 1939, just two weeks before war broke out, the spiritualist journal *Two Worlds* ran the headline 'No World War'. Nevertheless many terrified citizens turned to spiritualism during the Blitz air attacks of 1940 and 1941, looking for comfort and support. The appeal of

Extraordinary things happened at seances.

spiritualist churches was heightened because some mediums claimed to use their clairvoyant powers to predict forthcoming attacks. In the blitzed cities of London, Bristol, Manchester and Liverpool, their advice on whether raids were imminent and how to avoid danger was often taken very seriously. Assurances to those who attended that they would come to no harm in the attacks seems to have given many renewed strength and confidence to carry on.

In London an offshoot of spiritualism, the White Eagle Lodge, also became much more influential. It was based on the teachings of White Eagle, a native American spirit guide who communicated through the mediumship of Grace Cooke, the founder of the lodge in the 1930s. During the Blitz they distributed posters showing a 'cross of light' all over the capital. They were even displayed in underground stations where, every night, tens of thousands took refuge from the bombs. The posters supposedly helped protect shelterers by concentrating the power of thought and calling on eternal light. Many put them up in their houses believing they would protect them from a direct hit.

The greatest appeal of spiritualism – as in the First World War – was the promise of direct contact with relatives who had died in battle. Packed public meetings and 'home circles', made up mostly of women, sought messages from the nearest and dearest they had lost. Almost every week the spiritualist newspaper *Psychic News* published extraordinary stories of contact with dead soldiers, sailors and airmen. Its motto was 'life after death proved'. But as the influence of genuine spiritualist churches grew so, too, did the numbers of fraudulent mediums charging large fees for their services. A host of these set up businesses in back streets to cash in on the huge demand. All these claims regarding the supernatural aroused increasing hostility from established churches, especially some Catholics who saw it as the work of the devil. The government, too, was concerned to exercise control over activities which they believed might undermine morale or even breach official secrets.

Helen Duncan, Britain's
most famous spiritualist
medium. In 1944 she was
convicted under the ancient
Witchcraft Act.

This was the setting for growing official intervention and a campaign of police prosecutions.
The long forgotten 1735 Witchcraft Act was
revived and invoked against mediums on the
grounds that trance speaking and clairvoyance
were a form of 'conjuration'. The prosecutions
reached a climax in 1944 when the famous spiritualist medium Helen Duncan was charged at
Portsmouth Police Court with 'pretending to communicate with deceased
persons, to deceive and impose on His Majesty's subjects'. She had aroused
much official concern by communicating messages from deceased sailors
even before their ships had been reported to have gone down. The spiritualist movement believed that prosecutions like this were actually intended
to stop any leakage of classified wartime information. Helen Duncan was
committed to the Old Bailey where, after a trial and considerable publicity, she was found guilty and sentenced to nine months' imprisonment.

Since the last war, the influence of spiritualism has declined and until recently has remained
largely associated with the older generation. The
most famous post-war medium was Doris
Stokes, who introduced an easy going, conver-
sational style of communicating with the spirit
world, very different from the melodramatic
excitement of the Victorian seance. But, to the
post-sixties generations, spiritualism was widely
seen as too cosy, personal and family-oriented.
They preferred what came to be called channelling, in which mediums supposedly communicate with non-physical beings such as angels or
even extra-terrestrials. The messages are often
of general and cosmic importance, not the
family-oriented ones associated with spiritualism. Nevertheless, spiritualism played a key role
in the development of New Age ideas in Britain,
especially with its faith in the possibility of direct
contact with the spirit world.

During seances Helen Duncan
was said to produce ectoplasm
which took the shape of her
spirit guides.

TEKLA KHAN

My father came from a family of slaves and even in my father's day on the plantation things were very hard. And they all started to sing Negro Spirituals. It created a power to such a degree that they got the spirit people coming in, the old people that had died on the plantation. They all seemed to be very, very clairvoyant. My father said, 'Oh thank you God, thank you for sending the angels.' That's why he called it angelism. I was brought up with the idea of spirits and spirit people.

When I started to go to school – St. Anne's School in Stockport – nobody wanted to play with me. I remember, once, two children licked their finger and rubbed it on my face to see if the dark would come off. They said I had never been bathed, I was dirty, and they didn't want to bother with me. I was crying, I've never cried the same since, and I leaned on the school wall. Then I saw blades of grass growing through the bricks and I saw these blades of grass moving and it was then I first saw fairies. I didn't know what the word was but I saw these little people moving. I could see their little faces and I was so enamoured with that I thought it was just magic. Someone put their fingers into my shoulders and said, 'You should come into school,' because the bell had gone. And I was never afraid again. Those little people gave me confidence and I didn't care about anything.

Tekla was born in Stockport in 1905, the daughter of a plantation slave family. Her father was clairvoyant and was able to see the spirits of slaves who had died. Her parents left America and settled in Stockport where her father became a medical herbalist and her mother a dressmaker. As a child Tekla was able to see spirit people and had her first experience as a medium during the First World War. In the second war, she was accused of prophesying and prosecuted under the old Witchcraft Act. At the age of 93, she is Britain's longest serving spiritualist medium.

After that I started to see spirits. I remember I saw the spirit of our neighbour's Auntie Beattie who had died. I asked my father about this and he said, 'Now listen child, you and I and mummy, we can see people who come to us who have what everybody calls died. Some people call them spirits but we know they're angels. Nobody else can see them or talk to them.'

My parents went to a spiritualist church during the First World War and one day in 1917 the medium Mrs Laver hadn't come; my father nodded to me and I went onto the rostrum, where I gave clairvoyant messages. Everybody was very pleased and gave me sweeties saying, 'you're a clever child.' But my father said to me, 'you couldn't have done that by yourself, you did that because of the spirit people.' After that I was asked back to give clairvoyance again.

I didn't feel very different. In the north of England there was a lot of spiritual activity. Mothers would say to their children, 'if your granny ever says anything to you you'd better listen 'cos she's magic, she sees things.' In those days it was called the gift of second sight and most of the old people in the north of England had it. I had three spirit guides – Ramah, a little African girl called Zimba, she was wonderful, and Lancashire Jimmy. He was born in Oldham, he was very crude, and when he spoke it caused a lot of laughter.

I came to London at the beginning of the Second World War. There was a lot of interest in spiritualism there. Everybody of all religions would go to the spiritualist church because they felt they might find

Tekla's father was a clairvoyant on a plantation in Alabama.

out what was happening to their families, if they were going to be bombed. I was able to give them messages, very often from people who had been killed and passed over. When their loved ones were killed in the war, people wondered whether they were happy in the spirit world, so we were able to tell them. A lot of them became convinced through the war messages, more convinced of spirit return than ever before. Many people even left their own churches to join the spiritualist movement because it was comforting.

We got quite a lot of hostility from other churches. The Catholics often came in purposely to disrupt. They all said, 'you have no right to waken the dead.' Now that was quite amusing to me because the dead did not need to be wakened, they

Tekla: Britain's longest serving spiritualist medium. She first communicated with the dead during the First World War.

were already awake. They would say, 'you'll be damned you know, you're dealing with the devil'. Very often, wherever we were taking a meeting they would open the door and shout out 'spooks' and throw stones. They've done that and they've broken windows and sometimes rattled metal. Oh, it's been terrible.

It was very emotional for me just before the end of the war, because my eldest son's boat was torpedoed. Ken was very clairvoyant, he was a medium, too, and he'd gone right through and had his last leave when he told me that he was going to marry a girl he'd been courting, Doreen. It was devastating when his boat was hit. Eventually I got a letter to tell me the news but I already knew he'd gone. I was having a cup of tea one day, the dog was lying on the rug and all of a sudden the letterbox went and I heard, 'Yoohoo Mum,' which was the way he used to come when he came home and the dog jumped up and barked. My friend Lilly said, 'What's wrong with the dog?' 'Well,' I smiled, 'the dog's heard Ken. Didn't you hear the letterbox rattle?' She hadn't. I said suddenly, 'He's come home on leave.' She asked if I was going to let him in and I said he had a key, but he didn't come in. I opened the door and thought 'he's hiding in Nora's porch'. I looked but he wasn't there. I went to the corner of the road and looked down a side street, but nobody was there. I knew then that he had gone and that was how he'd come to tell me. It was about eight weeks before I got a letter from the Admiralty to tell me that his boat had been torpedoed and that he was feared lost.

I can never remember the word witch being used about me, but they always used to say, 'you've got the devil in you, it's only the devil that makes you do things like that.' Sometimes they used the word Satan. You could be prosecuted under the old Witchcraft Act for prophesying, it hadn't been used for many years but they brought it back in the war. The police would plant people at our meetings. I had one, a fake war widow who asked, 'are you going to read the cards or my palm or the crystal?' I said, 'nothing of this kind happens here, this is a spiritualist meeting.' But a few days later a plain-clothes policeman came to my door and said, 'are you Mrs. Khan?' I said I was, and he said, 'I've got a summons for you, you've been telling fortunes.' I had to go to Clerkenwell court, where the judge said, 'you have been purporting to get in touch with dead people and you are charged with prophesying, and prophesying is an offence.' At first he sentenced me to a month in prison. Then I was called back into court and he said, 'I'll rescind your sentence if you promise that you will never again try to tell fortunes from dead people and, above all, prophesy. If you agree, I'll let you off with a fine.' I said, 'I can guarantee, sir, I will never do these things again.' I was fined ten shillings. As far as I was concerned, I wasn't fortune telling. So I carried on taking spiritualist meetings as I always had and they never bothered me again.

GEORGINA BRAKE

I used to go round to my grandma and grandfather every Sunday and have tea with them. One day my grandfather said, 'I tell you what, Georgina, I've had two strokes and a heart attack. If I have another one it'll take me off. When I die, will you go to one of those churches and if I can come back and tell you I still live, then I will.' A fortnight later he dropped dead in his garden. After the funeral I said to my dad, 'you said you'd go to one of those churches and you haven't been.' Well, he took me along to a tiny little place – it wasn't a church really, it was a hall over the top of a Scout building. The medium was a lady, she came to my father and said, 'I've got someone here who says his name is Edward and that your name is Georgina. Is that right?' Well it was, and then she said, 'he's got something to tell you and that is – it's true, Georgina, I still live,' and that was the whole message.

We went home and told my mum and she said they must have known Grand-dad Edward had just died. Any rate, from then on they started seriously investigating spiritualism. When I was about eighteen, I went to a seance in Portsmouth, I sat next to a priest with a dog collar on. There was a Mrs Baylis from Birmingham who was the medium and you could see the beams of light coming from her tummy as she sat in the chair. She had a trumpet which the spirit guide would talk through. The spirit guide was an old soldier who had lost his life during the First World War. There were also a couple of children who were spirit guides. Curly was a little curly haired boy who had lost his life in a Zeppelin raid and Topsy was a little black girl.

Georgina was born in 1916 and grew up in Gosport, Hampshire. As a child she attended the local spiritualist church with her father. When she left school she became a dental nurse and it was at the spiritualist church that she met her first husband Ronald, a Naval officer serving during the war. They were married for just two weeks before Ronald was killed when a torpedo hit his ship. Georgina was heartbroken, her longtime friend Bob looked after her and following the advice of her spirit guide they subsequently married. However, it was not a romantic match, as Georgina had committed herself to rejoining Ronald in the spirit world. Georgina and Bob live in Huddersfield.

Georgina and Ron on their wedding day.

You each picked a flower from the garden and brought it to the seance and these were put in vases and the spirit children would play with them. We used to sing to raise the vibration, but on that day the main control of the circle said, 'I want you all to stop singing and listen.' We could hear a young boy whistling the Air Force march past, it got nearer and nearer until it was in the room with us, we saw a hand materialise and go down amongst the flowers, pick up a daffodil and bring it to the priest who was sitting next to me. He said, 'Hello Dad, it's Michael, my mother picked this flower from her garden this morning on the Isle of Wight, didn't she, and her tears are on it, but tell her not to cry. I'm with Grandma, I'm very much alive and I'm still learning to play the violin.' His mother was a violin teacher. So he said, 'we used to whistle this together Dad, will you whistle with me now?' and the priest whistled and the boy whistled in direct voice, it was a marvellous experience.

It really made an impression on me and after it was all over, I sat talking with the priest. They'd lost their son to meningitis about six weeks before this all happened. He said his faith didn't satisfy him, he didn't know what had happened to the boy, where he had gone, was it heaven? Someone suggested he write to a medium who had seances in her home which is what he had done. He was absolutely convinced and said he would try to put it over to his congregation that he knew that life was everlasting. It all made a terrific impression on me. Later, when I sat in on the seances that Mum had, I got to know a spirit guide called Chiefie who was a Native American Indian. I only had to ask him anything I wanted to know and if he didn't know he'd try and find out for me.

I started going to the spiritualist church in Gosport. There I met Ronald.

He was a very well educated person, who'd gone into the Navy after his father had died. He was quite a cheerful chap. We used to have biscuits and cheese and cups of tea together and then we started going out. We were sitting in a circle once when a guide called Faith came through; and she got hold of my hand, put it into Ronald's and said, 'I join two soul mates together in spiritual love.' Unbeknown to me, Ronald had long been in love with me, he'd never had a girlfriend, but he wouldn't tell because I had lots of friends, lots of boyfriends. But they weren't boyfriends you kissed and cuddled, they were just friendly with me.

Eventually, Ronald told me how he felt; then one day he said he was going away for two years to China and wanted to get engaged before he went. So we became engaged and wrote every day to each other for two years, so there were constant letters going backwards and forwards. Ronald used to write the most beautiful poetry. I've got some lovely poems that he wrote about his love for me.

During this time I was working in a dentist's surgery as a receptionist and nurse and there came a young man named Robert Brake. He worked as a technician and of course I got to know him quite well. He'd lost both his parents when he was nineteen; he was in digs in Gosport and not very happy. Any rate, this was the year before the war, the Munich crisis. Bob decided to join the RAF. By then, Mum had suggested that he'd be much happier lodging with us.

Bob introduced me to Handel's *Messiah* and the Gilbert and Sullivan operas. He was the perfect gentleman. He would take me out, realising the love between Ronald and me. He would hand me off the bus or the car and walk me to wherever we were going. One day I was sitting in the circle, when Chiefie came through and said, 'Sunshine, I want you to sit with the medium on her own so I can come and talk to you alone.' So I was sitting there with Chiefie and he said, 'Very soon you're going to have a terrible tragedy in your life and it will take all your courage to carry it. But it's your karma, my dear, and there's nothing I can do to stop it.'

I realised that it must be to lose Ronald in some way. I had to share this message with someone, and I shared it with Bob. I asked him to pray with me that at least Ronald would come home so I could say goodbye.

Bob and I went to a seance together and a lovely guide called Sister Hope came through and said, 'Sunshine, we know that you realise what's going to happen to your beloved but I want you to do something for me. It isn't our wish that you go through life alone – the one you call brother is my soul-mate; when we were on the earth together in a previous incarnation, he became a monk and so I became a nun. This time he's come back alone to live in the world. Will you take him as your life partner when you lose the one you love, to help teach him to live in the world?' So I said I would and I didn't tell anyone, not anyone at all of what I'd been told about Bob.

Time went on and, one day, there was a ring at the front door bell and there was Ronald on the doorstep. He'd become a petty officer and he was in officer's uniform. Ron wanted to get married, so we were married by special licence at St. John's Church in Gosport. Bob looked after the flowers. We didn't have anything fancy; we had a wedding cake, Mum had got a tea together and then we went home.

That was January 15th. We had a fortnight together and then Ron had to go on convoy to Scotland. On February 18th, there was a ring at Mum's front doorbell and in walked Granny Hill, who was Ron's mum, with a telegram in her hand. Well, I hadn't even had time to get the marriage allowance through and she got the telegram to tell us that Ron had been killed. Well, you can imagine, although I knew it was going to happen, it was terrible news. We sat with our hands on the table to see if we got a message and we got DEAD, dead, that's all. That he was gone. So then I told Mum and Dad what I knew, that there was nothing we could do, it was going to happen any how.

Of course, there was no funeral, no dead body, no nothing. I had nothing. Bob was wonderful. He came down every time he could to help me, to uplift me. About six days after it happened, a lady came to my door. Was I Mrs Hill? I said yes, why? And she said, 'your husband came through to our circle last night and he wants you to sit with me tomorrow afternoon. He gave me your address so I could find you.' So I went and Ronald came through, but it was only his voice. He told us that he was not drowned, he was killed. He had been asleep in his bunk and the ship came in and hit his head and killed him.

He said he saw a searchlight coming through the water and he went up to it. Chiefie and Ching Chong were there to meet him. They said he was to thank God for what had happened, as he would have died of TB, like his father.

I was overwhelmed and went to church every Sunday after that. Bob used to come home and we would sit together by the fireplace. When Mum had gone to bed, I would put my head in his lap and let out my broken heart. I loved Ron very dearly. Bob would put his arms round me like a brother and would comfort me. This went on for about a year and I thought 'well, I can't go on like this.' I wanted a child more than anything else, so I thought I might apply to a London hospital and see if I could look after children for the rest of my life.

I told Bob that I was applying to work in London. He took my hand and said, 'You can't do that, dear. I've been seri-

Georgina: looking forward to being reunited with Ronald in the spirit world.

ously thinking, more than anything in the world you'd love a child and I'd love a home. I don't ask you to love me like you loved Ronald, but I think we could have happiness together and we could have both those things.' Well, I thought it over. He was right, no-one else would understand my love for Ron like Bob. So the next day, I told my mother and Ron's mother and she said, 'Ron wouldn't want you to go through life lonely. He knew Bob and liked him.'

So we got married at Portsmouth Temple. I grew to love him within a few months after Ronald's death. I wasn't in love with him — that's something quite different — but I grew to love him because he was such a comfort. He's been a wonderful husband and a wonderful father to our two sons. We've had our difficulties but no rows, our understanding's too great for that.

BOB BRAKE

I was one of those who was never lonely but often alone. I was quite a serious young man. I remember Georgina had a happy, sunny disposition. She was called Sunshine in the circle in which she was known and she was a ray of sunshine. In fact, I once gave her a book which I inscribed: 'to Sunshine that has chased away my shadows' and I think that was it. She and I were very good friends, but love as I understand it hadn't come into it.

I knew the situation. Georgina and Ronald were very much in love. I knew Ronald, I'd met him a number of times. Georgina had told me of the message from Chiefie about a tragedy in her life. I was more or less prepared for something like that to happen. But it came quicker than I expected. I was stationed at Stanmore in Middlesex when I heard that Ronald had passed on. My first reaction was to go down to Gosport and see what I could do to comfort Georgina and help her. I'm glad I was a shoulder for her to cry on, if nothing more, at that stage.

On one occasion she said to me, 'well, the next time you come, I shan't be here.' She was going to try and get into nursing. I knew she longed for a child. Her short life with Ronald made that almost impossible and I wanted a home – subconsciously maybe – but there was that missing from my life. So I merely suggested to Georgina, 'I've been thinking, why not let us get married. I think we could make a go of it as companions, as husband and wife, you could have your child if we're fortunate enough; I would have a home and we'd make the most of what we have. You have lost a lot, I shall gain a lot – let's hope together we can make something worthwhile.' I couldn't love her like Ronald. I didn't have that fount of love within me that she had experienced, but I knew that I could care for her and I was the sort – decent sort, I hope – that would do everything to help her and so I made that proposal. She more or less accepted with the proviso that she got a blessing through spirit from Ronald.

Bob was born in 1913 in Romsey, Hampshire. He became a dental technician and joined the RAF in 1938. When he was demobbed, he worked for the civil service as a clerk. Bob and Georgina married in 1941 and had two sons, born in 1942 and 1948. They were warden and matron of a number of children's homes in Surrey before moving to Yorkshire to be closer to their own children. They have five grandchildren and one great-grandchild.

Bob: 'There was no jealousy on his part or mine.'

That came from Helen Duncan, the famous materialisation medium. We were invited to sit with her. Ronald came through and gave us his blessing and asked me to look after Georgina, and there was no jealousy on his part or mine. I just accepted it. It was something that happened and he gave me confirmation that I was doing the right thing.

Knowing that both of us were so definitely guided by spirit, we felt we couldn't go wrong if we appreciated and tuned into the spirit world because we were guided along the right pathway. I knew that eventually Ronald and Georgina would be reunited – by that time, of course, I had learnt of Sister Hope and that I had been a monk in a previous life and that she and I would be united. We had also been told that the time would come when the four of us would be together – Georgina and Ronald, Sister Hope and I. At the present time there are two of us in the spirit realms and two on Earth. But the time comes when you leave the earth plane and the four of us will one day be united. Well, that reassurance was enough to keep me going.

IVY SCOTT

My schoolmistress once said in front of the whole class, 'Don't listen to that Ivy Hazzard, she's odd.' I had strange visions. In one, I saw my Uncle Sidney being wounded and taken prisoner by the Germans during the First World War. I shook my head and thought nothing more of it, but word got round the school and my headmistress sent her condolences to Uncle Sidney's fiancée. She was furious and I was reprimanded for telling lies but a week passed and my Uncle Sidney didn't come home. They had news from the War Office that he had been run over by one of our ammunition wagons and taken prisoner. Then the visions stopped for a while. But when we moved to London I started to have terrible dreams. I used to dream of things before they happened. The only thing I ever got from my family was premonition of death and I can well do without that. When I was a little girl, I was once playing at

Ivy was born in 1902 in Weston-super-Mare. Her parents ran a theatrical boarding house and were very musical. It was while playing the piano to the guests that Ivy met her husband Jim. They lived in London where she worked in a railway office as a secretary and he was an engine driver. Plagued by health problems, Jim consulted a spiritual healer and the couple attended a spiritualist service where Ivy discovered her own clairvoyant abilities. She became a medium during the war at the height of the Blitz. She worked for the Spiritualist Association of Great Britain and at the College of Psychic Studies. Now aged 96, Ivy is Britain's oldest spiritualist medium. She lives in South London.

cards when I had a feeling that a man had just been killed and that turned out to be my father.

Before the Second World War started I had a terrible nightmare. I saw people with funny masks on their faces, crowds of people running down into the Underground. I saw lights exploding in the sky, buildings falling down and I thought whatever's happening? But things like that happened to me often and I would forget about them. Anyway, my husband was an engine driver taking troops down to Dover and collecting the injured; our boys had been evacuated and of course we all had to work.

One night I was exhausted when the siren went. I thought, 'I don't care if a bomb drops, it doesn't matter, the boys are safe.' I was lying sideways on the bed looking at the wall when, all at once, there was a hole in the wall. Through it stepped my father dressed in his busby and his scarlet coat from the First World War. He said, 'Come with me, my maid' – he was a Dorset man, he talked like that – and he went through what I thought was a tunnel. I followed him and when I got through to the other side – oh, the grass at my feet was like a carpet and I could hear the rustle of the leaves – it was twilight, so lovely. The movement of the leaves on the trees was almost musical and I said, 'Oh Dad, isn't it lovely here.' There was the sound of water in the distance and Dad took me to a fountain. 'Now I want you to cup your hands like you did as a child and splash your face with this water and to drink from it and tomorrow you will feel better.' I could taste the water as I swallowed it and feel the cool on my hands. It was wonderful.

I said, 'Oh Dad, the flowers smell so beautiful, I wish I could see this in daylight.' He said, 'If you saw this in daylight, Ivy, you wouldn't be going back and you must go back. You have a lot of work to do.' This was before I was a spiritualist. 'Oh Dad, I'm tired of work,' I said. He said, 'You'll soon know what I mean. No harm will come to you or the boys.' And then he led me back through the hole in the wall to my bedside. He disappeared and I fell asleep, slept like a log and the next morning I felt so different. Comforted. It gave me reassurance. I knew nothing would happen to us.

My husband Jim had terrible aches and pains so we decided to go to a spiritual healer and we thought it would be interesting to go to a spiritual-ist church too. So we went to the one at Clapham North, which was looked after by two elderly ladies and was covered in dust. The medium on the platform took one look at me and said, 'You should be up here with me.

You've been seeing things all your life.' I said, 'Oh, thank God, someone understands.' And that's how it started. I joined a circle in Bedford Hill, Balham. When it got to my turn one night, I was asked what I could see. So I went to one lady and what I saw over her head was a tangled string of thread. It was in such a knot, there was no way to undo it. So I said, 'all I'm seeing over your head is a tangle of string, a great big knot.' 'Well,' she said, 'my name is Mrs Knott.' We laughed and that night I went right round the circle with messages from the spirit world.

Once the war got going, we were hunting for places to comfort people. We'd meet in scout huts, we hired labour halls. It was lovely to see them coming from all denominations. Some were atheists, agnostics, but they were all desperate, they'd lost their loved ones and they were asked to

'I was an instrument of the spirit world.'

believe on faith alone that their loved ones go to heaven. We could prove, based on fact, the continuity of life, and that is the basic foundation of Spiritualism. The evidence used to be absolutely staggering. One young man came back, his parents were in the congregation and I said, 'Your son tells me to tell you he doesn't remember anything about being shot to pieces, all he remembers is that he flew his plane into the sunset and then, peace. His plane was destroyed over the sea, he didn't know anything about that at all.' And the wonderful evidence he brought back to his parents of what they'd done about his photographs and how heartbroken they'd been... They'd been looking through all the old photographs they had of him.

People came fearfully and in small handfuls, until the news got out and then we had to find bigger and bigger venues. I was an instrument of the spirit world. I would see clairvoyantly a soldier who belonged to a relative in the congregation. I'd get an impression of them from head to foot, because they

were pouring themselves into my consciousness and I could relay it to the loved one. Sometimes I'd become that person; then you get the full horror of what they suffered when they were wounded and died on the battlefield, and the agony they went through.

I remember I met a rather elegant lady one Saturday afternoon when I was at Ayr Street in Brighton. She wore brogues and one of those little trilby hats with the feather; she was sitting there and, all at once, I went up to her. 'There's a gentleman for you, he has a very military bearing. He asks me to say to you that you walked with the wind and the rain in your faces for one day and it was heaven.' She began to cry, then thanked me and said that she'd been waiting for that. She told me that they'd walked on the Downs, they loved each other but they couldn't break from their ties and they were faithful, so they had just that one day together.

There were people who weren't happy with what we were doing, but I didn't let that affect me. Opposite one of our churches was another church of a different religion, an established church, and they used to throw cans and bottles at the spiritualist place and shout abuse as we came out. Well, that wasn't very Christian. There was a lot of hostility. People would say it was the work of Satan and even from the spirit world I used to get men coming through to their loved ones and they'd say that if they were still on

Ivy Scott: 'the continuity of life is the basic foundation of Spiritualism.'

Earth they'd give me a witch's broom and a cauldron and a hat. But all we were doing was giving proof of the continuity of their loved one's life.

It was the evidence that started the crowds pouring in and then the spiritualist churches began to spring up. They'd work very hard and save money to buy a building and turn it into a church. Oh, and I remember the first Remembrance Sunday and how marvellous it was. It was packed out. My father, who'd been killed during the First World War, was working up on the platform with me. There was a gun crew that came through and I was one of the people who was blown up, and of course the relative was in the congregation and all you feel is a split second when you become that person. You just have to let it go and pass on the love to the family.

SHEILA KOTAK

The church we attended was run by a medium called Mrs Cooke, who was known as Mother to the congregation. This was during the blackout, so people took a risk in coming out in the evenings, but still they came and there were always quite a few people there. During the second part of the service Mrs Cooke would take several deep breaths and go into a trance. She would then be possessed by her spirit guide and so it wasn't her voice talking, it was the spirit guide – a little African girl who had died at the age of eight. As English wasn't her natural language and, because she was only eight when she died, she used to speak in pidgin language and Mrs Cooke's voice would take on a childish quality.

This was the time that the raids were very bad and it was near the centre of the city, so people were anxious about bombs and Mrs Cooke, through the little spirit guide, would give a 'blitz forecast', whether there would be raids that night or in the few days coming. She would say something like 'there won't be many bang, bangs tonight,' or sometimes she said, 'it will be very quiet for a while and today it won't start till late.' People certainly believed it so I presume the forecasts were reasonably true. My mother felt much happier if Mrs Cooke said through the spirit guide it will be a quiet night, there won't be much happening, or just a few bang, bangs tonight.

She told my mother once that she could protect all the people in her church but she couldn't necessarily protect their property and certainly my mother believed that. And as far as I know none of the congregation did get killed or badly injured, but at least one person was bombed out. We were living at the time in Kingsdown Parade, Bristol, quite near the centre of things, and for some reason it didn't have an air-raid shelter so during the

Sheila was born in 1929 and grew up in Bristol. Her mother brought Sheila and her sister up single-handed and took in typing to support the family. During the war they attended the Spiritualist Church in Sussex Place, Bristol. Sheila became a secretary in the 1950s and worked in professional offices around the city. On retirement she completed an Open University course and has just received her BA in Humanities. She is married to Pulat and has one daughter and two grandchildren.

Mrs Cooke, the medium, advised the faithful on when to expect air raids on Bristol.

blitzes we used to shelter under the stairs. It must have been fairly insecure but certainly the knowledge that Mrs Cooke could protect people was a great help to my mother and even to me as a child, too. It was a good feeling, when you were sitting under the stairs and there were bombs overhead and the house actually shook from an explosion nearby, it felt good to know that you were protected. There was a sense that whatever happened it wouldn't be too bad, that you would be alright.

YLANA HAYWARD

I remember when White Eagle used to come through my mother, there was always a lovely feeling of peace and strength. He had been a native American in one of his incarnations with a deep knowledge of Mother Earth. He was our guardian angel and brought a quality of love through his messages, to try and help mankind and also taught us about the power of thought.

Ylana is the daughter of trance medium Grace Cooke, who came to believe during the 1920s that she was in communication with White Eagle, a native American spirit guide. White Eagle gave many spiritual messages of light and hope and his word has since been spread by the White Eagle Lodge, founded in 1936, which is also a centre for meditation and absent healing. Ylana, the younger of Grace's two daughters, was born in 1916 in London. On leaving school she worked for the Lodge, graduating from secretarial work to editing the Lodge magazine, *Stella Polaris*. During the war she was inspired by White Eagle to launch a poster campaign featuring the Cross of Light in the Circle of Light, an ancient symbol which was regarded as a source of strength and protection. White Eagle, it is claimed, gave courage and inspiration to many in wartime Britain. Ylana lives in Hampshire.

The Poster of Light, which we had during the war years, was a wonderful source of strength to so many people. It was inspired by an address that White Eagle gave us which we called 'Let the Light Shine'. This knowledge of the power of light and how we could create that light through our own good thoughts, through seeing beauty, through envisaging the light coming, could bring so much good. He spoke of the cross of light in the circle of light and how if we envisaged it and realised the beauty of the symbol, it would spread across the whole country and protect us.

I was sitting on a tube train one day and I remember seeing with my inner eye a poster with the cross of light and the rays shining down with the words 'May the Forces of Darkness Halt Before the Cross of Light'. I had a strong sense that we had to have this poster made, so we started the poster fund and soon the posters were all over the place. So many people related subsequently the experiences they'd had about how they'd put the poster up and their house had not been bombed. There'd been destruction around them but their house had not been damaged. Lots of stories like that came to us, people wrote in to our magazine. One person said how they'd been walking with the poster rolled up in their hand and a bomb had fallen not far off, but they'd come to no harm. It just gave them a belief and a knowledge that all would be well and it was. They were even in the underground stations where people slept at night and we heard stories from there about how they were lying under that poster and the feeling of help it gave them.

There was a very strong sense that we were dealing with the forces of darkness. White Eagle was instructing us then, as a group, to use that symbol of the cross of light to push back, to protect from those forces of darkness. We used to visualise the symbol at our Sunday services and our particular work was holding Britain in the Light. There were many occasions during the war when we used it to draw attention to particular centres of need. With El Alamein, he told us to use this symbol to push back the forces of darkness, and with that working together with the British Army the forces of darkness did withdraw.

Stalingrad, I remember, was under great threat and White Eagle told us to concentrate very hard. There was a wonderful power we felt as we were doing it and the forces of darkness almost literally disintegrated then, but also, there were so many occasions when those we loved were in difficult, dangerous situations, that we were told to just hold them within the Cross of Light or the Circle of Light.

I felt the wings of White Eagle's personal protection, too. There was one occasion when my sister and I were staying alone overnight and the sirens sounded. We both of us got under the desk in the office and there was a wonderful feeling of calm that came to us as we just lay there. Then the sirens came sounding the end, the All Clear and we compared notes. We'd been so aware of the lovely feeling of wings around us, White Eagle was enfolding us in wings of light, and we just knew that we were safe. It

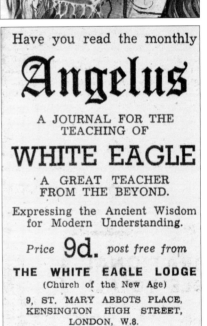

Have you read the monthly

Angelus

A JOURNAL FOR THE TEACHING OF

WHITE EAGLE

A GREAT TEACHER FROM THE BEYOND.

Expressing the Ancient Wisdom for Modern Understanding.

Price **9d.** post free from

THE WHITE EAGLE LODGE
(Church of the New Age)
9, ST. MARY ABBOTS PLACE,
KENSINGTON HIGH STREET,
LONDON, W.8.

was so frightening to hear the bombs falling, but we knew that all was well, all was well.

Then there was another, this other famous occasion when a firebomb fell on the roof here and a stranger came running in from outside and offered to go up into the attic. So up he went, he knew his way, put out the bomb, came downstairs, disappeared, we never saw him again. I still don't know to this day who he was. I sometimes wonder if it was an angel in human form.

During the Battle of Britain we were working particularly hard. One of our supporters was Lord Dowding who was very much involved in the Battle of Britain. I don't like to think of the Germans bombing Britain as the forces of darkness – they were like all humankind serving their country – but still it was the forces of darkness and, in a wonderful way, I think the Battle of Britain was won by the British forces helped by the power of the Light. We hoped it would encourage them to know that. White Eagle's guidance was that we were playing our part, doing our bit for the war.

BELOW
Ylana (left) with her niece Jenny.

OPPOSITE
People lying under the Cross of Light poster (to the left of the man sitting in chair) felt a special protection from Hitler's bombs.

ALTERNATIVE
WAYS OF LIFE

CHAPTER FOUR

I N 1898, Britain's first health food store opened in
Birmingham. Amongst the products sold in the
Vegetarian Food Depot were nut butter, banana
meal, vegetable soup tablets, potato flour and wal-
nut ketchup. Many of those who bought the goods
were people interested in alternative religions and unconventional lifestyles – pagans, mystics, theosophists, pacifists,
commune dwellers, naturists and early practitioners of com-
plementary health therapies. Vegetarianism was one important feature of an alternative way of life that was developing
in the first decades of the century. Vegetarians were lampooned as cranks,
marginalised, but, nonetheless, were pioneers of New Age living.

Vegetarianism has a long history, especially connected with religious and
ethical beliefs. In the East, many Hindu and Buddhist sects considered all
animal life as sacred and refused to eat meat. In Britain, it was associated
with radical, alternative religions like the Quakers and part of the animal
rights movement. The term vegetarian wasn't coined until 1847 when the
Vegetarian Society was founded and the nutritional benefits of a non-meat
diet were progressively revealed. Raw foods, it was suggested, had certain
living qualities which were conducive to health and well-being. But at the

OPPOSITE
*David Clement: 'before his time'
as an organic farmer.*

time there was still very strong opposition to the vegetable diet. The popular consensus was that no meat made you weak and, as late as 1878, a doctor writing in the *British Medical Journal* suggested that a vegetable diet could silt up the blood vessels with minerals.

The Vegetarian Society tackled prejudices by organising athletic events designed to break the public image that meat was essential for energy. The Vegetarian Cycling Club was founded in the 1880s, some of whose members held world records. Dr Allinson, who gave his name to wholemeal flour and bread, wrote that vegetarianism was the best diet for endurance sports. It was in the 1930s that the vegetarian diet began to gain the respect of nutritionists who agreed that people would benefit from eating a diet rich in fresh fruit and vegetables. Vegetarianism finally became more respectable during the Second World War when, with meat rationing, the non-meat diet came into its own. The Dig for Victory campaign encouraged people to grow vegetables and The Ministry of Food created cartoon characters Potato Pete and Dr Carrot, with slogans like 'Turn over a new leaf, eat vegetables daily' in an attempt to compensate for the lack of meat on the plate. In the 1930s, vegetarian Boris Pukatsch had been spurned by friends and colleagues because of his diet, but the tables turned during the Second World War when he was asked how to prepare vegetarian food.

Organic farming started in Britain during the late 1920s partly as a result of the demand for raw foods and nourishing wholefoods. The philosopher

Rudolf Steiner thought that modern intensive methods of farming overlooked the important spiritual aspects of the living world. He was convinced that there was another world beyond the physical and believed in nature spirits. Steiner became an influential figure in organic farming and developed a spiritual and scientific theory which considered the farm as a living organism. His ideas took account of the influence of the planets on seed germination and plant growth, abandoning the use of chemical fertilisers and promoting respect for animals as sentient beings. He suggested treating farm animals with homeopathic remedies. Steiner even anticipated BSE in the early 1920s when he claimed that feeding meat to herbivorous animals could make them mad. David Clement, one of Britain's first organic farmers, was heavily influenced by Steiner. He was regarded with mild curiosity in the early 1930s by his farming neighbours but, many years later, they told him that he was 'ahead of the times'.

FITNESS IN 1930

LET your good resolutions lead to good health. Include in your menu in the coming year food that will promote vitality and tempt your appetite. Protose and Nuttolene contain the rich well-balanced food-elements of new nuts; carbohydrates for increased physical and mental fitness, and energy. They are the perfect meat alternatives.

They can be made into any number of delightful dishes or served uncooked. They are easily prepared as pies and savouries; they make a ready nourishing dish for the unexpected guest.

BRITISH MADE.

PROTOSE & NUTTOLENE

Stocked in paper lined tins by all Health Food Stores

PROTOSE . . . . . ½ lb. 1/-;   1 lb. 1/8.
NUTTOLENE . . . . . ½ lb. 11d.;   1 lb. 1/7.

GRANOSE FOODS LTD., WATFORD, HERTS.

The adoption of natural ways also extended to health. One of the most significant aspects of the early New Age view was to promote alternative therapies. Amongst the new therapies they experimented with in the early decades of the century were osteopathy, chiropractice, homeopathy, the dowsing pendulum to treat diseased organs, Dr Bach and flower remedies and the Alexander Technique. One of the key ideas behind many of the therapies was to treat the patient as a whole. It was a holistic approach to health which considers emotional, intellectual and social factors as well as the physical symptoms. A significant date was 1928 when the Nature Cure Clinic opened in London. Run by a vegetarian and animal rights campaigner, it offered a menu of vegetarian foods, massage, homeopathy and acupuncture, the theory being that with plenty of fresh air, exercise and relaxation, nature will cure and preserve health.

Nature cures were one of the attractions of naturism when it took off in Britain during the 1930s. The medical profession had discovered that sunlight and fresh air were formidable enemies of the tuberculosis, rickets and rheumatism which were rife amongst the city slums. New Age pioneers were amongst the first naturists. They celebrated the body, taking pride in it and rejecting the traditional restrictive notion of the body as being something to be ashamed of and covered up. The naturist movement was largely German-inspired and was part of a growing awareness of physical culture that included sun- and sea-bathing, long hikes and organised physical exercise. For those interested in alternative religions and beliefs, this return to nature had an additional spiritual meaning.

As increasing numbers became interested in alternative lifestyles during the early decades of the century, certain locations started developing as New Age centres. Some of the places to draw these pioneers were Britain's

An astrologer demonstrating what was claimed to be the horoscope of Christ during a conference on astrology in Harrogate in 1939.

sacred sites. Most popular of all was Glastonbury with its ancient religious associations and alleged mystical powers. In the 1920s, Alfred Watkins claimed to have discovered the existence of ley lines and formed the Old Straight Track Club. He organised walks to Glastonbury – amongst other places – to experience the power of ley lines. St. Michael's ley line was said to pass right through the Glastonbury Tor, traditionally viewed as a magical place. For eighty years Glastonbury has been the focus of many a New Age pilgrimage. The first Glastonbury Festival to attract people was not at Worthy Farm in the early 1970s – in fact it took place in the 1920s and was organised by the composer Rutland Boughton.

The most popular of all the alternative beliefs amongst early New Age thinkers in Britain was astrology. Astrology derived from the belief that there is a correspondence between the positions of the sun, moon and planets in the 12 zodiacal signs and physical, mental, spiritual and emotional well-being. By ascertaining what the map of the heavens was like at a person's birth, it was possible for an astrologer to gauge the prospects for good health, love or fortune. Astrology clubs, such as the Libra Club in London, opened their doors to amateur enthusiasts in the early 1930s.

Astrology reached a mass audience in 1930 when it made its first appearance in the popular press. The astrologer R.H. Naylor was invited by the *Sunday Express* to cast the horoscope of the newly born Princess Margaret Rose. He did so predicting 'events of tremendous importance to the Royal Family and the nation will come about near her seventh year'. In fact, her father George VI acceded to the throne a few months before her seventh birthday. Naylor's article was a success and he was invited to write another. In it he suggested that British aircraft might be in danger. On the very day of publication, the airship R-101 crashed in northern France. Naylor became famous overnight and went on to write regular columns that were copied by other newspapers. The 1930s were the Depression years, characterised by high unemployment and growing uncertainty, and many people turned to their horoscopes for clues as to what the future held. By 1941, the Mass Observations Archive reported that two-thirds of adults read their horoscopes in the daily newspapers and that four out of ten had some degree of belief. Astrology had reached the mainstream and become the most visible face of early New Age Britain.

Kathleen Keleny-Williams

I was terribly fortunate as a child as I was lucky enough to have vegetarian parents. When my father was 18 he moved to Birmingham and joined lots of different clubs and at one he heard a lecture on vegetarianism and thought, 'Well I must be a vegetarian myself.' He got together with four friends, who were also vegetarians, and they thought how wonderful it would be if they could take this vegetarianism to other people. It just so happened that there was a building to let on Corporation Street and they said, 'Let's take it and open a vegetarian hotel.' There were no other vegetarian cafés in Birmingham then and the hotel was tremendously success-ful, they often had over 100 people for lunch. Then people wanted to take vegetarian food home with them, so they started a food depot. This was food for health. My father suddenly thought 'food for health – health foods', that was when he coined the term; the first health food store start-ed and very soon they were all over the country. He then realised that his real work was to manu-facture for the stores, so he bought a building and set up a health food factory. That was in 1908, the year I was born.

Kathleen celebrated her 91st birthday this year and feels that her life has never been fuller. A lifelong vegetarian, she attributes her good health and vitality to her diet and lifestyle. Her father opened Britain's first vegetarian hotel in 1908 and coined the term 'health foods'. Kathleen followed in his footsteps, running a health food shop in Coventry before the war and then moved to Gloucestershire to start her own vegetarian guesthouse. Today Kathleen's son and daughter-in-law run the guesthouse and she lives in a flat next door. Kathleen still grows most of her own food, practises yoga daily and is an active member of the Vegetarian Society. Despite losing two husbands Kathleen believes that she will never be lonely so long as she has her piano and garden.

As a child, therefore, I was brought up vegan. I had a very happy childhood and never had a day away from school for illness. I loved being out of doors, I always walked to school, rode my bicy-cle and helped my father in the garden. At school, when children asked me why I didn't have school dinner, I said, 'Well, I don't like eating meat, so I don't eat animals.' They said, 'Oh we don't eat ani-mals, we love animals,' and I said, 'But don't you have meat?' To which they'd reply, 'Yes we have the ordinary meat at school.' 'Well, that's animal.' And they said, 'Is it?' And they'd go home and ask their parents, who then had quite a job persuading them to eat meat for dinner. To me it seemed shock-ing that people could eat meat, that horrid stuff that comes out of the slaugh-terhouse. I couldn't believe that any health could come from that.

Because my father was a keen vegetarian he belonged to the Vegetarian Society. As a child I was often taken to meetings with him and I remember a talk on Tolstoy and hearing the words that Tolstoy said: that the slaughter-houses were chambers of horror where the bodies of animals were spoilt, where the souls of men were spoilt because they were having to kill all day long, and ultimately where the spirit of a nation was spoilt.

Another great influence on me was Mahatma Gandhi. When Gandhi came to England, my father was asked to provide the food. Gandhi lived by the motto 'Ahisma' and I thought that's just what I ought to teach myself, 'Ah' meaning not and 'hisma' meaning hurting. Not hurting anything, any creature, any person by word or deed, or thought.

I grew up, then, feeling that the vegan diet was absolutely right. The food we ate was not at all limited, my father made nut cream, nuts ground very finely, and later almond cream, which was beautiful, and then whole-meal bread. We never dreamt of having white bread and white flour; in fact, we used to say white flour was very good for mixing with water for sticking up wallpaper, but you didn't want sticky gluey stuff inside you like that. This diet meant that I was never ill. As I child I didn't have any of the illnesses, chicken pox or measles, that other people had. When people ask what illness-es I have had, I answer none yet; not real illness-es, thank heaven! So I am so pleased that I came to vegetarian and vegan parents and could be brought up on the right diet not having to kill anything, any animals at all.

I had lots of friends when I was young but I never thought of marrying any who were meat eaters; one was simply not interested in marry-ing a meat eater. One day I met someone at a con-cert, I saw him once or twice afterwards and he said, 'D'you know I've got a confession to make to you.' I said, 'Oh yes' – I thought of quite a few things, what on earth could it be? Then he said, 'I'm afraid I'm a vegetarian.' Then I saw him in a

Kathleen's father: the man who coined the phrase 'health foods'.

different light altogether. He was someone that I was interested in. He was a good walker and a keen talker and believed in what he said. We had the same views about religion and so eventually we married and lived happily ever after, right till he died.

When we married, my husband and I set up a health food shop in Coventry. We used to sell all sorts of things there, Allinson's flour, bread and scones; all kinds of dried fruit, especially dates and prunes and figs and apricots; lentils and wholemeal macaroni; and then we had nuts, brazils, cashews, almonds, walnuts and kernels. When Coventry was bombed during the war we had to leave and we ended up moving to Gloucestershire and opening a vegetarian guesthouse at Coombe Lodge.

Besides being vegan, I also started to practise and teach yoga and many of the guests joined me. One thing I had learnt as a child was to walk barefoot on the grass first thing every morning. It is so lovely in the morning when there is still a slight dew on the grass, walking barefoot on it you can feel the earth giving off its magnetism and energy. Every muscle is focused in the soles of the feet and, by walking on the dew, one gets the energy and vitality which lasts you all day. Besides walking on the grass, I used to go to the trees and hold the tree with the fingers around it so the centre of the hand is against the tree. That's where the energy and healing comes through the hand from the tree, and, first thing in the morning, when the tree is sucking up its food from the earth then it shares its food with you, its energy and light. At first, when guests came to Coombe Lodge they just looked through the windows but the next day they were all out there, going through the grass, and very often in the winter you'd see little tiny foot marks in the snow.

I have always been a keen gardener. My father was, too, and I loved working with him. I liked to listen to what he said; he told me it was important to grow things organically – the word organic wasn't very popular when I was a child. It seemed terribly wrong to poison the earth by putting artificial manure on it, as the earth is not ours, we can have a garden but it is only lent to us. Voltaire once said that perfect happiness comes when you have your own garden and can cultivate it for yourself. I still have my garden. I try to grow all my own vegetables organically and I know the pleasure it brings me.

At 91, Kathleen still grows some of her own food.

BORIS PUKATSCH

The very idea of killing animals and eating their flesh was a horrible thing, and certainly in the Mazdaznan philosophy it was said that animal flesh would taint the blood. I was brought up in the Jewish faith and I discussed with my rabbis the ten commandments and 'Thou Shalt Not Kill.' They said that it only applies to your fellow men, but I said rubbish. At the bottom of my street there was an abattoir, I used to hear the animals crying and it wasn't easy.

In the Jewish faith, you ate a lot of chickens and fish, it was an abomination to me.

My parents would give me a live chicken, put it in a bag and I had to take it to a certain place where they'd remove it from the bag – a live hen – pull the feathers out, cut its throat, let the blood run down the drain and put the near-dead corpse in your bag to take home. It was a nasty business.

Boris became an ethical vegetarian during the 1920s. Abstaining from meat was also part of the Mazda philosophy, an Eastern belief originating in Persia which laid great emphasis on a healthy diet and exercise. Boris has been a Mazdaznan since the 1930s. He found that being a vegetarian was unattractive to women and has remained a bachelor.

I started thinking that it couldn't be right, eating all this meat and fish and animals. By some chance, I met up with some young enthusiasts who persuaded me that I would be better off giving up that sort of thing. I never looked back. I was an ethical vegetarian right from my teens. It seemed to attract me and I met some young people who were members of the

Vegetarian Society who were also members of the Mazdaznan philosophy. I used to go to functions, I used to go to parties, I was a young man but the food that people ate, I wouldn't touch. I was near-vegan and it sustained me and if people thought it strange, it didn't bother me.

I was working in a big factory before the war, Burton's. The people there used to rag me occasionally; when it came to meal times, they'd throw a lettuce leaf on the floor and say, 'that's for you Boris,' but it didn't really matter to me.

Of the ramblers and cyclists I went out with, not all knew I was a vegetarian. I didn't smoke or drink either. We would cycle twenty five miles and stop for a break and then someone would hand the cigarettes around. I would just say no, and if I'd already dated one of the girls, they'd look at me and say, 'you don't smoke.' Later we'd call in at a pub, and they'd all order beers and I'd have a lemonade. The girl I'd dated would look at me and say, 'you don't smoke and you don't drink, hmm.' But the crunch came when one of the boys had a windfall on the horses, betting, and he treated us to dinner in a restaurant. So we all went in and he said we could have anything we wanted. Somebody had pork pie, some had steak and chips and I said, 'I'll have a salad.' This one girl whom I'd dated looked at me and said, 'You don't smoke, you don't drink – don't tell me you're a vegetarian?' I said 'I am a vegetarian.' 'Right, the date's off. I want to marry a fellow that's got red blood in his veins.' That didn't upset me, because it was the pattern. I just got used to it.

But when the war came around the boot was on the other foot. We had to start growing our own food so parks were turned over all over the country and tons and tons of vegetables were being produced. It was fantastic: there was lettuce, carrots, tomatoes grown indoors, outdoor crops like peas and beans and these things were reasonably quick and easy to grow. We dug up turf and used the virgin soil underneath and within a few months we had fruit and vegetables to sustain us.

I gave away my meat coupons and got a cheese ration instead. Those people who wanted meat three times a day had a hard time but I never had that problem. Ministry of Food broadcasts on the radio encouraged us to eat vegetables. There was Doctor Carrot and Potato Pete. That one talked about the virtues of potatoes – how to mash them up, use them in dishes, that sort of thing. Well, of course, I had a head start over all of the meat eaters.

There were lots of recipes that you could do using a potato base, mashing it up with scraps of bread, lentils and left-overs. They would all be put into a deep fry and we had some marvellous cutlets, tasty with salt and pepper. The neighbours used to walk in and ask for recipes for things that you could do with vegetables. They might have thought me odd in the past but they could see that I was mobile and healthy, so it opened their eyes a bit. I was never short of anything and after a while I wasn't a crank any more.

DAVID CLEMENT

Our ideals were to grow the best quality food for man and beast. Straightaway, we made Broome Farm into a self-contained unit. A farm should be a balance – the right number of crops and the right number of stock for the land. It was like a symphony. The balancing of crops and stocks is a wonderful thing. We had cattle, sheep, hens, geese, pigs. We fed them all ourselves, we didn't buy in any food. It's great to get the right relationship of grassland to arable land and it's a completely fascinating system because every animal lives also on the waste of another animal. We tried our best to be self-supporting which no farm did in those days – everyone did what was cheapest but we tried to feed our own animals completely which nobody else was doing.

Because we accepted the idea that nature spirits were a reality, we treated everything in nature with more respect. We knew we were dealing with spirits as well as physical things which made us appreciative of what they did. The gnomes work upon the roots, the undines upon the leaf and stem of the plant, the sylphs upon the flower and the salamanders on the forming of the seed.

David Clement was one of Britain's first organic farmers. In 1933 he bought a farm near Stourbridge and adopted Rudolf Steiner's philosophy of bio-dynamic agriculture during a decade of increasing mechanisation of farming. The aim was to supply nourishing organic food to Sunfield, the neighbouring Steiner community for disabled children. David's approach to farming was influenced by a strong belief in nature spirits.

These spiritual beings are life, they are the beings that push up the plants out of the ground. They are difficult to experience today because we are far too materialistic in our outlook, we imagine that everything is physical but in the old days people experienced them.

With nature spirits in mind, we were more thoughtful in what we did, we were cautious. When it came to harvest, we used to cut with a scythe around the cornfield and we'd gather up all the corn in sheaves and lay them on the hedge. Then, when the reaper and binder came in, there was a patch cleared and they would cut – nothing was wasted – and when the field was cleared we'd bring our geese or the women would come in and glean.

The whole plant world grows through the benefit of the sun and the moon, but Steiner said that all the planets have an influence on plant growth in subtle ways and that the whole farm had to be a complete organism in itself. The waxing moon is a tremendous germinating force and the sun force gives quality. Steiner explained how to use these and he gave us various preparations which we could spray on the land and place in the compost heaps. We composted all our manure and vegetable stuff and we put certain preparations in them which have the power to bring these planetary forces into activity, into actual manure so that it enlivened everything. We endeavoured to promote life in everything.

The animals definitely were sentient beings, they have souls and we treated them with respect and

OPPOSITE
David Clement: 'Animals have souls and we treated them with respect and gratitude'.

gratitude for all that they provided us with over thousands of years. One always strove for harmony on the farm, a feeling of well-being. One

of the nicest jobs in winter was going to rack up the cattle at night in their yards, with straw, hearing all their heavy digestive noises as they lay there comfortable and knowing that all was well. When there were diseases, we used homeopathic remedies on the cattle; for an eye disease we added drops into their water trough and it worked. We've had good results with scour in pigs; in fact, we found homeopathy exceedingly helpful.

The children from Sunfield benefitted from the food. We grew our own wheat, ground it, milled it and baked it. I've never eaten bread again that was as good. We grew our own potatoes, our own fruit and had our own eggs and meat and even cheese before the war. It was nearly all vegetarian food, little meat was eaten. I'd never eaten vegetarian food before and I enjoyed it immensely because it was so well done and varied.

In the early days, other farmers looked upon me as a peculiar chap, but when I came to sell the farm on retirement, one said, 'You know, you were before your time.'

ALBERT SUTCLIFFE

Albert was born in Bradford in 1917. Both his parents were mill workers and his father also worked as a fishmonger. His mother was a spiritualist and all through his life Albert has had psychic experiences including a strong sense of having had past lives in ancient China. Albert became a noted theosophist as a young man which led to an interest in the subjects that theosophy fostered including yoga, astrology, Eastern religions and naturism. He was a pioneer of body culture in the 1930s when the prevailing attitude was that the sight of bare flesh was offensive. He lives in Bradford and has one daughter.

I'd always been interested in outdoor activities and, as a boy scout, I'd done a bit of camping. When I was older I got a bike and joined the Cyclists Touring Club and spent most of my Sundays pedalling around the Yorkshire Dales. I had also been a member of a wrestling and weightlifting club and got interested in physical culture. I wanted some outdoor activity and when I saw an advert in the paper for the 'Yorkshire Sun and Health Association in Formation', I thought that might provide a bit of camping or there might be people with similar interests to mine, so I replied. A man got in touch and it was only then I discovered that it had anything to do with naturism. I'd always been interested in going to the local lido and swimming and sunbathing, so this club seemed to offer everything that I'd been looking for, and there was this addition of nature.

We had an inaugural walk so that people on the list could get to know each other and then we decided to have a meeting in Leeds to start the club, so that willy nilly I found myself part of the Naturist movement. There was a book called *It's Only Natural* and it was very influential. We found a site near Holmfirth, a beautiful place, but the weather was terrible up there. We went up to inspect it and then we just stood around the flat place where we were going to pitch tents and one of the ladies said, 'Oh well, we'd better make a start' and so we did. Everybody took their clothes off, we all sat down and went on with our conversations and there was no feeling of embarrassment – that was an artificial thing that had been thrust on society during the Victorian era. Occasionally, when members got talking, you'd find the odd one who'd say, 'When I first came I was petrified, but then when we took our clothes off and everybody else was unclothed I felt perfectly at home.'

I loved the freedom of it. Swimming was great without clothes, especially in those days when there were so many woollen swimming costumes which always stayed soggy for hours. There was great liberty in swimming without clothes on, you'd feel the air and the wind on your body. It was sort of new and radical. I mean in that era the human body was supposed to be a very wicked thing. On the stage, they had nudes but they weren't allowed to move. The naturist magazines never showed any pubic hair.

'In those days the human body was supposed to be a wicked thing.'

We would sometimes take a walk down the river in Harrogate. There was a stretch which was not on the public walkway and the only person you'd find there was the occasional angler. We'd play games throwing discs over a net. We also did exchanges with other clubs. We visited the Hull Sun Society. I remember it was a cold, wettish day when we went to the Lancashire Sun Society near Preston. I didn't really tell my friends what I was doing, but I don't think they would have thought me a crank, they would have thought I was lucky.

OLIVIA ROBERTSON

Glastonbury was a magnetic centre. It drew many people, myself included, going way back, because of the Tor and all of the wonderful Avalon stories of King Arthur. In the 1940s, I used to stay with my uncle who was a vicar up on the Mendips and visit Glastonbury. It was here that I had mystic visions, once, of the Holy Grail. There was the paganism of the tor, the dragon rising up. I remember druids telling me about that, the dragon power in the earth and the Archangel Michael who embodies fire. Then you have the sacred well, the Chalice Well with its legends of the Holy Grail and so there was this wonderful mixture – paganism up on the tor and Christianity centring round the Chalice Well and both here in harmony. The ley hunters had come here in the 1920s, they declared that there was a network of ley lines right around the tor and this drew psychic visionaries as well as archaeologists and religious people on pilgrimages. Spiritual people felt rainbow coloured light coming from the tor.

I came here as a VAD nurse during the war when we felt that Britain was about to be invaded. With others we felt, somehow, that we must surround England with light. We had Coventry bombers flying right over the vicarage and occasionally dropping bombs. I was busy sending out white light power, pure light of love to protect the British Isles. So Dion Fortune and all – witches, black magicians, white magicians, pink magicians – were all united in saving this island in the Magical Battle of Britain. The silent minute sprang, we all prayed at nine o'clock when Big Ben struck. We felt we were using occult powers to fight somebody who was using occult powers against us. It did seem supernatural and I believe helped Britain to save herself.

In 1946 an extraordinary vision changed my

Olivia Robertson was a 'pioneer hippie' during the 1940s and '50s and one of the pilgrims drawn to the emerging New Age centre of Glastonbury. Olivia grew up in Ireland, where her family were friends of the poet W.B. Yeats, who revived interest in Ireland's spiritual heritage and faery lore. She was a cousin to Robert Graves whose book *The White Goddess* described the pagan idea of a Goddess. From early childhood she had psychic experiences and believed she was in touch with nature spirits, the dead and other-worldly beings. She kept her visions secret and became a best-selling novelist until, in 1946, she believed she had had a mystical encounter with a Goddess which transformed her from a bespectacled author into the colourful Goddess worshipper she is today at the age of 81. Her vision led her to found the Fellowship of Isis, an international neo-pagan organisation dedicated to promoting the Goddess. The Fellowship has since been recognised by the World Parliament of Religions, the first Goddess-based organisation to achieve this. She lives in Ireland in her family's ancestral home, Clonegal Castle, located on a sacred site with many magical associations.

life. I had a vision of a Lady, she was made of crystallised white light, had raven hair pulled back into small dark curls. Her form was smooth, her arms bare and her dress appeared to be without any seams, made up of strips of pale green and lilac material. She had an amazing mind, a superior mind. I instantly knew that I was in the presence of a Goddess, because of the power of her concentrated thought. She had a mind far beyond ours. I was so embarrassed thinking silly things and she could hear every word. She sat down on a chair facing my bed, her arms folded. We spoke for about half an hour but the strange thing is I can't remember what she said. Finally, at the end of our interview, the Lady rose to her feet. I noticed the glorious way she moved. The walk was unearthly, beyond human. She said that she had to go away. Now, with spirits it is generally inferred that they appear and then, their visitation concluded, dematerialize. But I gathered from telepathy that this Lady had to wait for some sort of aeroplane. I couldn't understand why a spirit would need a vehicle, but I had a very strong impression that this aeroplane would take her to a huge ship as big as the Queen Mary or bigger, that sailed high in the sky.

Such an experience took me over the threshold of belief into knowledge that beings exist beyond the physical world. I knew that the Lady was as real as myself and not an hallucination. I had found the Goddess. This

completely altered me because up to then I'd had very short hair, spectacles, I wore tweeds, and no make-up in the country: and no nail varnish. I was very county, large shoes, ankle socks, a highbrow novelist. I was respectable and now I ceased to be that – to people's amazement. I grew my hair and did it up the way the Lady had, with sort of long tassles. I never knew I had so much hair. I started wearing bright colours and make-up. As I did this my friends began to as well, and you could say we were pioneer hippies of that period. We became more creative and my writing completely changed, the language was much more romantic.

Glastonbury, spiritual capital of New Age Britain.

Gerald Pitchforth

When I came down from Yorkshire, I discovered that London had so much to offer. I wanted to study palmistry and so I went to this chap who was a palmist to the royalty, he was a top man at that time. So he took me on and owing to my unusual hand – I've got the life line and the head line in one, everyone else has got a separate head and heart line – this chap's view was that I needed a little more balance and that I was too sensitive. The one thing he recommended was to go into astrology, and from that moment on I began to investigate it.

I discovered that there were many astrology groups operating around Baker Street. The one I joined was called the Libra Club. Each week we put up the birth map of one of the members there. On one occasion, an elder-ly chap put his horoscope on the board and explained to us that he'd had certain bad config-urations and he'd had a mild stroke or two. He told us that he was expecting his next bad config-uration and his next stroke in a few days' time and he didn't think he'd survive it. So that night he shook hands with us all and said, 'I don't think you'll see me any more.' Off he went and in fact that was exactly what happened.

Gerald was born in 1901 in Yorkshire and moved to London to work as a bank manager in 1932. A shy man with a stammer, he consulted a palmist who suggested that an interest in astrology could make him less reserved, so he joined the Libra Club in Baker Street. During the war, Gerald served with the Royal Engineers and returned to banking afterwards. A lifelong bachelor, Gerald is now Britain's oldest astrologer and casts charts to help him play the stock market. He lives in Bournemouth.

It was a small club and it took only about ten or fifteen people per night. There were all kinds of people – housewives, a dental surgeon. Peo-ple were feeling the need for additional infor-mation then to help them plan their lives. It gave clues that you got nowhere else, it told you things that you knew nothing about. The funny thing is that I never did stammer when I was talking astrology, I think that when you're talking about something you're really interested in, you overcome your sensitivity.

After the phoney war, when the real war came, all the clubs closed down. The banks were asked to release a certain percentage of staff for the war and I was one of them. I didn't want to be in the Pay Corps, so I visited a clairvoyant, she was a well known woman there in London, and she had four pieces of foolscap paper and a pencil. Off she went into a trance where

Gerald interrupted his job as a city banker when he was called up during the Second World War. He offered his services as an astrologer to the War Office.

she was engaged by the Master called Johannes. He was her spirit guide and she told me that he would answer any questions that I had. He asked for all kinds of information about what kind of a chap I was, and eventually it came out that I had to go and be a water diviner, and that would keep me out of the Pay Corps. So I practised divining every Sunday morning on Hampstead Heath. Eventually I got into the Royal Engineers and they used me once for my water divining. A bomb had dropped onto the Marie Curie Hospital and they sent me there with my divining rod to try and find radium. I went to a chemist's one day and found out what radium was – it's a bluish liquid – but I didn't find any there.

I was working at the Institute of Civil Engineers throughout the war and, after a while, I decided that really astrology should be looked into, as I thought that it could help the war effort in some way or other. At that time I didn't have an exact plan, but I did think that the configurations in the sky do indicate certain things and that we can use that knowledge. So I conveyed this to my commander in the unit and he sent a note to the War Office. A message came back to say that they already had an astrologer, Louis de Wohl, and he was working in Grosvenor House. Apparently, he was giving the War Office the same horoscope as Hitler's astrologer was giving to Hitler, and they were using this knowledge to try and get an idea of what Hitler might do next. I was invited to go in and meet de Wohl, but I said that well, if he's working there, there's no need for me to go there too.

HEAVEN ON EARTH

CHAPTER FIVE

I N 1898, a group of idealistic young anarchists left their homes in south London to return to the land and build a utopian community in a remote part of the Cotswolds. Inspired by the writings of Tolstoy and his vision of the Brotherhood of Man, they bought forty acres in a windswept spot in Gloucestershire. This was to become Whiteway Colony, Britain's longest surviving experiment in communal living, which has recently celebrated its centenary. Today, the descendants of the utopian pioneers live in comfortable bungalows and are employed in a variety of jobs in the area. But when the experiment began it was truly revolutionary in purpose. The aim was to create a self-sufficient community, living independently of state and society. One of the pioneers' first acts was to abolish the use of money and to burn the deeds of the property they had purchased. Most remarkable of all, Whiteway was just one of a number of communes and alternative communities which flourished during the first half of the century long before the heyday of the 1960s.

There is a long tradition of communes and utopian communities in

ABOVE
The bakery of Whiteway Colony in Gloucestershire, Britain's longest surviving experiment in communal living.

OPPOSITE
Bruderhof member in the 1930s: they looked back to the radical ideals - and dress of the Anabaptists.

The Bruderhof community settled in the Cotswolds during the 1930s. Their aim was to lead a simple life of practical communism.

Britain, beginning with the attempt of Gerrard Winstanley and the Diggers to build a heaven on earth in the mid-seventeenth century. Since then, the thread of these alternative back-to-the-land communities can be followed through the Quakers and the religious sects like the Moravians and the Transcendentalists. In the first decades of the twentieth century, a number – like the Cokelers in the village of Loxwood in Sussex, the Plumstead Peculiars on the Kentish side of the Thames and the Abode of Love in Somerset – still survived, inspired by a strong spiritual and religious purpose. In the 1930s, the Quakers continued their tradition of back-to-the-land experiments with the land settlement movement, an idealistic attempt to resettle unemployed families from the cities on communally owned farmland in counties like Gloucestershire, Wiltshire and Northumberland.

A number of these communal movements found inspiration for their alternative life in the biblical teachings of the Sermon on the Mount. One such group was the Bruderhof, formed in 1920 in Germany, which fled Nazi persecution and set up a Cotswolds base near the village of Ashton Keynes in 1936. Their aim, looking back to the radical ideals of the Anabaptists in the sixteenth century, was to live a simple life of practical communism. There was no private property. Work was organised on a communal basis, with job rotation so that the most menial tasks could be shared. All meals were eaten together and the children were cared for communally from an early age.

Another group, similarly inspired by the fraternal principles of the Sermon on the Mount, were the members of the Brotherhood church which was formed at the end of the last century. In 1921, they established a Christian anarchist community on a plot of land in the village of Stapleton near Pontefract in Yorkshire. Disillusioned by the First World War, they aimed to build a haven of peace and communality, quite separate from the society and the state which they believed was responsible for this mass slaughter. Their maxim was and still is – to live by the rule of love, not the rule of law. But this soon led them into direct confrontation with the state. The founders had no planning permission for the wooden houses they built in the 1920s and the local council demolished them. The men were frequently imprisoned for their refusal to pay taxes and the women imprisoned for refusing to register the birth of their children. The Brotherhood was a very small community, consisting of just a few families, but remarkably they remained and rebuilt their homes.

The spiritual and religious impulse to form alternative communities was coupled with a romantic one. As industrialisation transformed Britain into an urban society, blighted by poverty and class division, the rural idyll of a simple and wholesome life held a grip on the romantic imagination. The dream of traditional craft-based communities living co-operatively, close to nature, which inspired William Morris and the arts and crafts movement, remained a potent force into the early twentieth century. One of the best known pioneers was the artist and designer Eric Gill who set up three arts and crafts communes during the inter-war years at Ditchling Common in Sussex, Capel-y-ffin in Wales and Pigotts in Buckinghamshire. Arts and crafts ideals were very much in evidence at the Whiteway Colony in the Cotswolds. It established the Cotswolds Co-operative Handicrafts, making and selling a variety of goods like sandals, boots, leatherwork and furniture.

Members of the Whiteway Colony pooled their skills and resources to build the community.

Love and sexuality were key issues in many communes. Attitudes ranged from puritanism to sexual libertarianism. Brotherhood members rejected conventional marriage as it involved the state and the established church. Amongst the Cokelers, marriage was abolished as it was thought to interfere with the spiritual relationship between the individual and God. The Bruderhof disapproved of any form of birth control.

Whiteway was the most libertarian of all, though its reputation for sexual experimentation was greatly exaggerated. By the 1930s it had achieved local notoriety as an immoral and promiscuous community. This was prompted by the general rejection of marriage in favour of free unions based on love. Its reputation was further blackened in the eyes of locals by the presence of a few naturist residents and a fairly relaxed attitude to dress — bare chests and sandals were a common sight on Whiteway in the summer. By the standards of inter-war Britain most parents were extraordinarily liberal in their sexual attitudes. They were unusually open, telling their children about sex and, as they grew older, advising them on birth control. To a large extent the liberal sexual attitudes worked and most partners remained together in lifelong free unions. Some of the younger generation, however, growing up in the 1930s and '40s, rejected the sexual libertarianism of their parents and chose the conventional path of marriage.

One of the principles shared by almost all the communities was pacifism. Some of the commune dwellers were imprisoned during the First World War, but in 1939 the state took a much more liberal approach to conscientious objectors. They could get exemption from military service if they worked for the war effort. As farming was a reserved occupation, those communes that grew crops and kept animals – as many did – could be seen to be involved in legitimate war work. Remarkably, as a result, the war led to a growth in alternative back-to-the-land communities, swelled by conscientious objectors who registered as agricultural labourers. The commune movement was given even greater momentum by the Peace Pledge Union, the main pacifist organisation in Britain, which urged pacifists to bear witness to a higher order of morality by joining co-operative communities that might act as seed-beds for a new civilisation.

Most of the young men and women who joined the communities during the war years were pacifist idealists. Many were middle-class and they usually came from the towns and cities truly hoping to build a rural heaven on earth, a shining example to a war-torn world. These ideals fired the imagination of those who arrived in communes like the Elmsett community, based on a 41-acre farm in Suffolk. The new commune dwellers adopted many of the principles which had inspired the pioneers. They tried to be communal, pooling their resources and sharing everything, even sometimes sexual partners. They also experimented with ideas that were to become far more popular after the war: at Elmsett, for example, organic farming methods were practised and there was a commitment to equality between the sexes. From March 1941 onwards *Peace News*, the newspaper of the Peace Pledge Union, began publishing a monthly supplement devoted to life in these alternative communities.

The reality, however, rarely matched up to the ideal. Many of the commune dwellers had little or no experience of farming and found their spartan life on the land very difficult. Sexual experimentation often did not work and the division of labour remained deeply entrenched with the men in the fields and the women, for the most part, engaged in domestic work. Some groups like the Bruderhof became rigid and dogmatic in their attitudes. There was often hostility, too, from family members, from local villagers and from the state. Those commune members who refused to officially register as conscientious objectors were imprisoned. In 1941, fearing punitive state action, most members of the Bruderhof emigrated to form a new community amidst the tropical jungles and grasslands of Paraguay, leaving behind the old world for the new.

After a few months or years, most of the commune members drifted back to the towns and cities. Some had lost their idealistic vision, but more often they wanted to get married and bring up their children in a more conventional way. When the war ended so, too, did most of these alternative communities. During the war they had a common enemy – a nation at war – but with the coming of peace, their differences of opinion often became intolerable, and the communities broke up.

While most of the long established communes were fading in post-war Britain, their members choosing the comfort and convenience of a more affluent urban society, a few began new communities. The first and most successful New Age community formed after the war was in 1962 at Findhorn on the north-east coast of Scotland. The founders, Dorothy Maclean and Eileen and Peter Caddy, achieved worldwide fame by growing giant vegetables on an arid plot of land, using no artificial fertilisers. They believed the garden grew because guidance from God enabled them to communicate with nature spirits. Soon Findhorn became a place of pilgrimage for those wishing to practise organic gardening and share in the deeply spiritual way of life established there.

From the late 1960s and through the '70s there was a new interest in back-to-the-land communal living, inspired by the hippies and the counter-culture. A new generation of utopian idealists dropped out and returned to nature, hoping to create a better life than that on offer in the cities. Most were unaware that they were part of a radical tradition in Britain going back to the beginning of the century and before. For, despite the conventional wisdom that communes were an invention of the hippies, there were probably more alternative and experimental communities in Britain during the 1920s and '30s than there ever were during the counter-culture of the 1960s.

Doolie Keele-Wolfe

Whiteway started as a small group of people who wanted to try this alternative way of living. We didn't believe in governments, we didn't believe in marriage, we wanted to be self-supporting, we were trying to do it without money. So the first ones wandered around until they found this piece of land up on the Cotswolds which they thought would be the right place and, between all of us, we managed to raise enough money to buy it.

Everything was done communally, the men worked the fields and the women did the cooking, there was even sharing of shirts and things like that. We solemnly burnt the deeds because we didn't want anything to do with governments. There was no religion in Whiteway, either.

Doolie was born in 1923 and spent her teenage years in the free-thinking, liberal environment of Whiteway Colony in the Cotswolds near Stroud, one of the oldest communes in the country which recently celebrated its centenary. During the war she joined the Land Army and worked on a farm. Her stepfather was in charge of finding work for war refugees and it was through him that she met her first husband, who was a refugee from Italy. She has lived in Italy and Ireland but returned to England when her husband died. Subsequently she met up with an old friend from Whiteway, Tom Wolfe, whom she later married. Doolie is a mother and a grandmother and lives in Cheltenham with her many animals.

For me, as a child, it was complete and utter freedom. Everybody knew everybody, all the kids played together, we had freedom to go over the back down the fields to the woods and catch crayfish. There were big communal picnics, we used to go down to the stream to paddle. There were no restrictions on us children. You could go to anybody's house, no-one locked their doors at Whiteway and it was usually auntie this and uncle that. There was no formality. Money just never changed hands. You never charged for anything. When we had a 'do' on at the hall, everybody brought cakes, they brought sandwiches and there was a collection, but it was all a question of not paying for things.

We definitely felt we were different and I think we were proud of the way we lived. We thought it was the right way. But a lot of people got the wrong idea about Whiteway – they thought we were a lot of communists but it wasn't true. I mean: there were people with different ideas, all sorts of ideas and there were a lot of pacifists too.

We also tried to get away from the idea that we were a nudist colony because we were not. There was one woman who lived near us, and you'd often meet her walking around with just a hat and sandals. She was the only real nudist I knew. But a lot of people did sunbathe naked in their gardens. My stepfather often wandered around in the nude: in fact, my mother made him a tiny codpiece because she didn't want him walking around completely naked. But he insisted on doing the gardening in this thing and nobody worried. People did wear very little in the summer and we liked going barefoot. We were not ashamed of our bodies, but didn't flaunt them. I remember a friend once telling me about a conversation he overheard on the Stroud bus between two old ladies, talking about Whiteway, one saying it was a nudist colony and that the postman had to undress before he went there.

We used to get coach trips, excursions coming to see us – what they thought was a nudist colony – and there was this lady, Flossie Davis, who did teas and they used to stop and have tea. Then they'd stop at the top of the hill and you'd see them looking around; we kids would go up to the bus to talk to them so they'd throw pennies out of the window. We'd run to pick them up with our toes to make them throw more.

My parents were very, very liberated. When I started having boyfriends they were quite open, they told me about sex and to be careful. When I was sixteen or seventeen, my boyfriend often stayed overnight at home and they had no objections at all. I just can't remember a time when I didn't know about sex and there was nothing shameful about it, it was all to do with love. My parents were very loving to each other and very loving to me and it all just seemed perfectly natural. They taught me about what we called in those days French letters, which was really all there was in those days and that's the one thing I knew when I started with my first boyfriend.

He was one of about six or seven refugees from the Spanish Civil War and the hall had been turned into a dormitory for them. They were all these handsome-looking lads with their dark eyes – they couldn't speak any English. They were a great attraction not only to us young girls but to some of the older women as well. I liked this one and made a bee-line for him, we got pally and he was my first sexual experience. I told my father that I had – and they had no objection, they just told me to be careful, to make sure that he did use a French letter, because they said babies were conceived in

'We were not ashamed of our bodies, but didn't flaunt them.'

love, only in love. That was one of their ideas: that you didn't just go around having children. You waited until you met the person you really loved and then you had children, which was what I did.

Many of the older people did not believe in marriage. There were a lot of partnerships, they called them 'free unions', and they didn't believe in anything to do with officialdom. They thought that marriage wasn't necessary – if you had a good partner to live with, you just lived with them. All the free ones that I knew of were together like my parents – and quite a lot of them worked out very well.

Looking back, for me Whiteway was Utopia. I knew we had some cranky people there and I knew people thought we were cranky, but I thought the other people were cranky. For me it was THE place to grow up; it was the place where I was happiest, with this big community which was a family, in which there were no worries, no fears as a child. We were normal people who just had our freedom more than other people.

*'We were proud of
the way we lived.
We thought it was
the right way.'*

David Randolph

For a small child, Whiteway was idyllic. There was a great deal of freedom for us children to roam and most parents devised some means of calling us to meals. My call was a cow bell which could be heard up to half a mile away. We lived in two corrugated iron ex-army huts which were especially constructed for the tropics. My father had bought them from a Government auction sale at the end of the First World War but they were very cold in winter and burning hot in summer. The community itself was set up using Tolstoy's teaching about communal living in the open air. People were free to think their own thoughts and willing to work together in harmony and without conflict. They thought at first that they could live without money and produce enough vegetables and things to barter but this soon proved unworkable.

David was born in 1918 and is Whiteway Colony's oldest veteran. His father Stanley, a conscientious objector in the First World War, dropped out of medical school to become a sandal-maker and took the family to live in a craft-based community in Holt, Norfolk before becoming one of the earliest members of Whiteway during the 1920s. David lived at Whiteway until the 1940s when he rebelled against his parents in his desire to be ordinary. He became a furniture maker and was a farm worker during the war. He married Elizabeth in 1941.

There had been a grandiose scheme to start up a boarding school with children from all over. That lasted about a year but it wasn't a success, there just weren't the facilities. Later, when I was of school age, they started another one. We had conventional lessons in the morning and the afternoons were taken up with crafts: pottery, woodwork, leatherwork, bookbinding and music as well. It was a glorified playgroup really, fine for a child of six, which is what I was by then, but we soon slipped behind and didn't keep up with the normal curriculum that a child of say ten was getting even in the village school. So from then on it became a big drawback, academically it was a big loss. Others took their children out of the school. My education definitely suffered.

The people at Whiteway looked different. At that time very few people, especially in a rural district, took their shirts off to work, but at Whiteway the men wore shorts in the summer and went bare-chested. This was frowned upon by the adjoining villages. From early childhood, I wore a smock and little short trousers, but as soon as I left the Colony to go to the post office, the village boys would poke fun and rough me up because we were different and children don't like being different.

The Randolph family in 1922 outside their first round hut home in Whiteway.

LEFT
David Randolph aged 19.

We were vegetarians virtually from birth. The diet was very frugal. We had nut milk to drink which wasn't very palatable and butter made from various nuts like hazelnuts. It was only when we started to go out into the world that we realised how difficult it was to be a vegetarian in those days, especially when you went into lodgings, so you went pretty hungry at times.

Part of the free thinking was free

Whiteway School picnic in Sheepscombe Woods, 1930.

David: found he wanted a more conventional life.

loving and if you wanted to go and live with someone you just did. My father was attracted to a suffragette called Maud who wasn't interested in a sexual relationship and then he got to know her sister who was to be my mother. The relationship between my father, my mother and Maud was always a bit of a mystery. My parents lived together for a very long time and had children before they eventually married. My father professed to believe in the freedom to love whoever he wished and this caused a lot of problems in the family as we were growing up.

He had a relationship with a young schoolteacher. She lived in our house for a time. Neither my sister nor I approved of it and we could see that it was hurting my mother. She never complained, though. She came to accept that she'd just have to grin and bear it. There was nothing we could do about it, he was determined to have his own way, but I think it contributed to my mother's ill health.

It had an effect on my relationship with Elizabeth. I had seen what irresponsible relationships could do within a family. I wanted to be fairly ordinary from my early teens onwards, I wanted to conform. Elizabeth would have accepted a much freer union but I insisted that we did the proper thing and get married. When I started to mix with people from outside Whiteway, I began to wish for a more conventional life. It seemed to me to be more ordered to have conventions to live up to. I gained a lot from Whiteway but the idealism never really transfers from one generation to the next. Once I'd left childhood my belief was always that you never go back, you always must move forward, whatever it brings.

Elizabeth Randolph

I was raised in the East End of London, the only daughter of a man who'd come out of the First World War with a determination that we were going to build a new Britain, that they weren't going to go fighting any more, that there was going to be peace. So I was brought up to be independent, looking towards a new Utopia, not only in England but a brotherhood of man in the world in general.

I came away from a war-torn London during the Blitz. My home for nineteen years was very badly damaged and my father had had a nervous breakdown, so I took my parents off to live in Gloucestershire. I got a job making cartoon films where I formed a friendship with a girl who came from Whiteway. We teased her because she wore sandals, no make-up and was a vegetarian, but when I went to Whiteway for the first time I found this friendly group of people to be like a big family, which I'd lost in London. It was like a little Utopia, especially having come to the countryside from a blitzed East End.

You could live very freely at Whiteway, it was very much 'hats off, sandals on'. The atmosphere was very informal and people treated each other as equals. Even the children called the grown-ups by their Christian names and this was in the 1940s. Most of the older men didn't shave and their hair was fairly long in a sort of

Elizabeth was born in London in 1921, the daughter of a baker who became Labour mayor of West Ham. As a young woman she attended Peace Pledge Union meetings with her father. The family home was destroyed during the Blitz, prompting Elizabeth to flee to Gloucestershire where she worked as an animator for Anson Dyer studios on the Dig for Victory campaigns. She became a land girl in 1941 and moved to Whiteway Colony in 1943 after falling in love with David Randolph, a member of one of the early commune families. After the war she trained as a nurse and eventually became matron of a welfare home. On retirement she developed a small business buying and selling antique furniture. Elizabeth and David have four children and live in Westbury, Wiltshire.

David insisted on getting married, although Elizabeth would have been happy with a free union.

Jesus style. One or two of the women wore kerchiefs and beads. Everyone was considered when decisions were being made. Once a month, there was a colony meeting when people decided what needed doing, whether it was rebuilding the dry ground, something on the roof of the hall or somebody applying for a piece of land.

When I started dating my friend Rosemary's brother, I expected him to arrive in a farm cart, but in fact David drove up in an MG sports car. There were a lot of free relationships on Whiteway pre-war. It was the avant garde thing to do. There were several couples who had interchanged their relationships; and my own parents-in-law lived together and had children for many, many years before they married. I was quite keen on the idea of us living together for a year or so to see if it would work, just as people do today, but David didn't want that. He felt that if we were going to go outside to work in the conventional way as farm workers, then we should be Mr and Mrs so that no questions were asked. We had enough problems as it was, being conscientious objectors, without inviting more questions.

People in Stroud were a bit suspicious about Whiteway. When we descended on the town like the barbaric hordes with our sandals, long hair and in our unconventional clothes, the story going round was that there was a lot of free love which meant illegitimate babies. We just lived together and had sex and, at Christmas, sorted out the babies and divided up the children. Of course, that was all rubbish but it kept the local people happy and we all laughed about it.

In 1943 we applied for a piece of land and built our own house on Whiteway. I already had one baby about nine months old and was pregnant with another. It was rough country living. We didn't have any water because we hadn't dug our own water pit so we had to rely on rainwater and when it was dry weather we had to go three miles away to Miserden to fetch water in a drum. Every drop of water had to be used so if I washed a lettuce out in rainwater, I kept it to do something else. It was difficult with small babies because everything had to be done by hand, like the washing, and there was no refrigerator to keep the babies' milk fresh. We had oil lamps, a big kitchen

range and wood had to be chopped. It was very tiring pushing a wartime pram over the rough stones. I fell into a severe depression so much so that I couldn't even lift a knife or fork to feed myself. It was put down to the war, people thought it was because I had gone through the Blitz, but I wonder if it wasn't some form of post-natal depression.

Later I realised that I wanted to bring up the children in the conventional way and for them to go to a good school, so we decided that we must go and work in a town and get back to a normal life. Whiteway for me was not so much a success but it did open my mind. It gave me a broader idea of life altogether, it was an education.

Elizabeth Randolph and friend with their children during the 1940s. 'The story going around was that there was a lot of free love and illegitimate babies.'

Hilda Gibson

Hilda as young mother.

We lived by the power of love and justice rather than by obeying a law because it was a law, that's what the ideals of the Brotherhood were based on. We were pacifists, we lived off the land. We felt that the teachings of the Sermon on the Mount were about loving one another, loving your enemies and the contact with Mother Earth was a furtherance of that, because we're all part of the same thing, whether we're human beings, animals or plants.

After the First World War many in the community wanted to start afresh, make a connection with Mother Earth and they sought to buy a piece of land here. They wanted nothing to do with deeds. The first house to be built was the community house, but the local council got to hear about the building and said, 'Huh, these people have built these houses without planning permission.' We said, 'This is God's land, we don't need planning permission, we built these houses for ourselves to live in, not to be sold.' They pulled down the first house. It was rebuilt, causing a lot of inconvenience and difficulties, people living in sheds and hen houses and things like that; it was built again and they pulled that down, and the original community house, and took away the materials to pay for the cost of demolition.

But we built them without planning permission because we did not recognise the laws that said planning permission must be sought. We refused to ask for permission from a murderous State that we had no respect for, a State that had killed thousands, millions of people in the First World War. They had no morals. This is what I grew up with, and every six months or so, when the rates were due for the houses that were pulled down, the heads of all the households on this field were taken to court because they hadn't paid the rates. I

Hilda was born in 1929, the daughter of one of the founding families of the Brotherhood Church, a Christian anarchist community in Stapleton near Pontefract, Yorkshire. Her husband Len was a conscientious objector who was imprisoned several times and told 'with your barmy ideas, you should join the people at the Brotherhood Church.' He settled there after the war and together Len and Hilda strive to maintain the principles of the Brotherhood Church, living with as little involvement by the state as possible. They try to be self-sufficient, growing their own vegetables and keeping a cow. On arrival at the commune one is greeted by a notice-board which gives a topical message relating to peace and justice in the world. While Len and Hilda are now the only resident members of the Brotherhood Church, they have many supporters amongst their family and friends who visit the community to celebrate special occasions. Their most regular visitor is their new grand-daughter, Katie Saffron, who gives them a sense of continuity and hope for the future.

remember the police coming to arrest my father and the other men because they refused to pay a fine and they went to prison on a regular basis from when I was a baby until 1936. They accepted the punishment of the State for which they had no respect.

We didn't break laws for the sake of it. We felt that we weren't going to kowtow to a law that was not related to the essence of truth and love and that each man and woman is an entity with a right and a responsibility to think for themselves. Some got married without a Registrar present. My parents got married in a ceremony that was similar to a Quaker meeting where people sat around and made their declarations that they were going to be husband and wife. That's how we got married, too, the attitude being that it was a marriage of minds and hearts and love, and with God. We didn't feel that it had anything to do with the State.

My brother and I, our births weren't registered because our parents didn't believe in it and I was prosecuted for not registering my eldest son John. I said, 'It's not their affair, these children are our children and we will bring them up the way we feel is right and when they're old enough to make their own decisions they can.' I got a conditional discharge, four shillings costs. It happened again when the twins were born and they were going to send me to prison and take the twins from me because I wouldn't pay the fine. It wasn't a question of dodging, it was that these children weren't handed over to the State within six weeks of being born.

We believed in love as a way of solving all problems and treating everything on this Earth correctly. That's why we did not talk about pesticides, herbicides and fertilizers, all we did was put lime on the land and manure. We believed that all the creatures have a place, all the plants have a place even though we hoed the weeds out. We lived off the land, kept

ABOVE
Hilda (second from right) during the 1960s. 'We believed in love as a way of solving all problems.'

BELOW
The Brotherhood church buildings were put up without planning permission. The local authority demolished them.

bees and did organic gardening and we really believed that we had to treat the soil right, respect it and not use poisons on it. The land is a living thing and it must be treated in the same way as any living thing. There's always a strange feeling of peace when you come to this piece of land, and I feel that's because of our spiritual approach to life and because we've buried our dead here. From the start, we were building up a little heaven on earth and I'm thankful I was brought up like that.

Norah Allain

My husband and I were pacifists. Roger had actually deserted the French army where he was doing his military service and come across to England as he just couldn't stand it any more. We of course got into difficulty as his position was illegal and he couldn't get a job, so we ended up spending a year on Dartmoor in a little cottage lent to us by friends of mine. While we were there we took a magazine – *Fellowship of Reconciliation*, I think it was – and there we read an article about the Bruderhof. This was a community consisting mostly of Germans who had been forced to leave Germany and English people who had joined since they had been here. They welcomed people who were interested to come and visit them. This sounded very good and so Roger went off, hitch-hiking to the Cotswolds Bruderhof and stayed there for a few days. He came back very impressed.

I was naturally rather adventurous. I was also a pacifist. I didn't exactly belong to any particular church and I was rather open minded on the question of religion. This meant I was slightly worried about the Christian basis of the Bruderhof, but I was willing to look at anything that seemed to provide a solution for us. So I went along to the Bruderhof taking our first little son with us, he was only a few months old then.

When the Second World War broke out Norah was 24, a young mother living with her first son and her French boyfriend, Roger, in a remote cottage on Dartmoor. Her father was a schoolteacher and she herself had been to university in London. Both Norah and Roger were pacifist and at the outbreak of war they learnt about a community called the Bruderhof in the Cotswolds which welcomed conscientious objectors and strove to create a peaceful, Christian and communistic heaven on earth. After two years with the Bruderhof, they emigrated to Paraguay to set up a new community. Life in Paraguay was hard. Norah, like many of the other women in the Bruderhof, had lots of children, one of her babies died in the early years in Paraguay. Norah, Roger and their 11 children left the Bruderhof in 1961 and went to Brazil. Widowed in 1991 Norah still lives in Sao Paulo. Her children are multi-lingual and the family spans the globe. Norah sees herself as a citizen of the world and is still a seeker, open to new ideas and spirituality.

Visiting the Bruderhof for the first time was really something. I remember the sight of them sitting round eating in a great big dining room, they had talks during the meals and then singing together and dancing together. It appealed to me very much. It was very moving to find people enthusiastically all together.

What also attracted us was the ideal of people of various nationalities and even colours, all living together in brotherly love. There were Germans, Swiss, Dutch, French and a lot of English. Of course, they were not an average cross section of society – a lot of them were people who'd already been to college but not all, some were quite simple people. But all were very idealistically inclined and anxious to do something completely contrary to the war atmosphere. This was a community in which everyone gave up all their belongings and put everything together, to live a simple and better life. We definitely felt that this kind of community could represent a pattern which eventually humanity could follow. That was the idea and if we joined we would be making a witness for this fact.

ABOVE
Community dressing: pinafores and polka dot scarves for the women.

BELOW
The Bruderhof did not believe in birth control, and Norah had 12 children.

So the decision was made to join and a condition of joining was to bring everything we had and give it to the community. We went back to our cottage and fetched our few belongings. That consisted of very little. I think we had thirty pounds left, we had been living on next to nothing, my husband hadn't had a job and so we just had some savings. A great deal of stress was laid on not having anything personal, so I even gave up my watch. I noticed later somebody else wearing it.

When we arrived we were given so much more, though, everything was prepared beautifully for our little baby and us. The baby went to the baby house and was looked after by people who were trained in looking after babies and so I knew he was safe. This freed me to join other departments and work and meet other people. I do remember being a bit sad that I didn't see much of my husband. Before, we had been living together and seeing each other all day long; now, he went off to some work department,

The Bruderhof community lived off the land.

I went to another. We saw each other for a short time after lunch but then again in the evenings there would often be meetings after supper and so one didn't have very much time together. That was at first a bit difficult for me, but we got used to it.

When you were new to the community and enthusiastic your one desire was to get rid of your own old clothes and be given the Bruderhof costume. This happened when they were convinced that you really wanted to stay and become a novice. We women wore very long dresses right down to the ankles, voluminous from the waist downwards, a tremendous lot of cloth. We had a pinafore, or apron-type garment, tied round our middle, and then we wore a white blouse underneath it and had a polka dotted scarf which we tied around our neck. The men wore something which was not quite so distinctive, but it was mainly black, and wore a type of breeches to just below the knee and stockings up to their knees.

For women, being a mother was seen as the most important role. As a result of the attitude to birth control, basically that you didn't use it, we all had as many children as came naturally. I had twelve, so did very many of the other people. This meant that for about twenty four years of my life I was practically pregnant or feeding a baby all the time. The Bruderhof took great care of mothers. When the time came, after the baby was born you were left for two weeks in the mother house, being taken great care of. Visitors were allowed, but not immediately. You were given one day of peace and quiet when only the husband could visit and then other friends and children could come. After that you went home for four more weeks in which you looked after your baby at home and your other children in the evenings. After the six weeks were over you took the baby to the baby house and went back to work. I was happy for my children to be looked after by people who were properly trained and enjoyed doing it.

This apparently so perfect brotherly life did not of course always turn out to be quite perfect. If you came up against any difficulties, you had to confront the person with whom you were in disagreement and efforts would be made to put it right. To some extent this worked but there were certain problems which didn't go away. There were inequalities. I noticed that special privileges were given to the members of the original founding family and also to some of the early members who had joined in Germany. I noticed they were getting a few extra perks, I couldn't talk to my husband about it,

as he wasn't interested. I eventually got so upset that I actually ran away. I was feeling desperate because, you know, everything was not as it should be if, really, we were all equal in brotherhood. I didn't have any plans as to where I was going, I didn't even know the countryside. I think I'd never been outside the gates, so I just went off into the country and walked and walked most of the day. I was seven months pregnant. Then the night came and a soldier on a motor bike saw me and picked me up and left me at a police station. They questioned me, found out where I'd come from and rang up the brotherhood.

When I ran away I had no rational plan in mind, I simply did it because I was desperate and wanted someone to take notice. It worked and we addressed my problems.

'This was a community in which everyone gave up all their belongings and put everything together to live a simple and better life.'

By then plans were being made to emigrate to Paraguay. As the war went on, everybody was becoming more and more conscious of what was happening and eventually we heard that there was quite a lot of antagonism felt towards the community by the surrounding people. Not only were there a lot of Germans who were not yet interned but also English people who were pacifists and had not joined the war effort. Understandably the local population were not happy. So there came the question of our emigrating. A couple of brothers went to Canada to see if we could go there but Canada didn't want pacifists, then they went to the States and again it didn't work, they didn't want us. Finally they arrived in Paraguay, the male population of Paraguay had been decimated by an earlier war and they were keen to welcome immigrants.

I was thrilled to bits with the thought of going to Paraguay. I had always had the idea that I would like to leave England and go to some bigger and warmer country. The idea of going away was wonderful.

To begin with, life in Paraguay was extremely hard, making a new community in primitive conditions with the heat, disease, and mosquitoes. But what was important was putting the ideal above the material circumstances. It made you willing to put up with any difficulties and we put up with an awful lot. We definitely felt that our kind of life would be a model which

'The community started to change… the original ideal had been lost.'

eventually humanity could take. Unfortunately, towards the end of the 1950s, the community started to change and we felt that the original atmosphere and ideal had been lost. The Bruderhof had grown around the world and slowly, in Paraguay, we felt that we were being used in a larger power struggle between the different groups within the Bruderhof. Hierarchy became more important than deciding as a group, and the final straw for us came when Roger was wrongly accused of going against the good of the community. As long as it lasted I felt that I was really doing something which was good for me, from which I learnt a lot; but when the time came, both Roger and I knew it was right to leave, to go some other way.

Noel Hustler

In 1939, before war was actually declared, I found myself in the middle of Ipswich handing out leaflets which argued that people should give up military force and honour the pacifist approach. It just so happened that there was another young man there, distributing similar leaflets. He gave me one and said, 'I live in a farming community of conscientious objectors and pacifists, we think this is the right way to build up life anew rather than go to war and kill people.' He then invited me to come and see the community in the village of Elmsett just outside Ipswich, which indeed I did. And that was how I first heard of Elmsett.

I was barely eighteen at the time but my ideals were clear. I did not want to kill anybody with firearms and I did not want to starve to death any member of any population. Wars had never succeeded and the way of life expressed by the military had never resulted in creating a peaceful and happy society. There must, I felt, be some other way. At Elmsett they believed that if they could build up small units of communities throughout the land, they could create a nation which would rely on a loving and peaceful approach. There is no doubt that Elmsett was set up in the belief that our way of life would produce a finer society, a happier society and a healthier society. Even as a young man I knew that the factory life, the way we produced our food, the educational way in which we were all pushed into straitjackets of belief, was wrong and that there must be some better way; a fresh way of approaching our lives, a happier way, if you like, and indeed I found that happier way at Elmsett.

I was always a rebel but when I gave up my job and joined the community my parents were horrified. I was, however, of an independent mind and I

Noel has always been a rebel. Born into a middle-class Ipswich family in 1922, he won a scholarship to the local boys' school. He came close to expulsion on several occasions, but the final straw for his parents came in 1939, when rather than going to university he joined the newly established pacifist community at Elmsett. After five hard but blissful years at the commune, he left with his new wife Margaret to follow a career of caring for young offenders. Eventually he made up for his parents' early disappointment by becoming director of social services in Bexley, London. Today, Noel is a Quaker and lives with his wife Margaret in their home in south London. The sociable and liberal atmosphere of Elmsett lives on in their home, where they welcome a constant flow of visitors made up of their children, foster children, grandchildren and friends from every part of the globe. Despite Noel's later respectability he maintains an air of rebelliousness, recalling his time at the Elmsett commune as 'the best time of my life ever'.

was determined to do what I felt was right for me, for my friends and the society around me, and if that went against family tradition, that was just too bad. It meant that I was cut off from my cousins and my aunts and everybody connected with my family and if they saw me cycling through the town, they looked the other way, they didn't want to know. I was totally rejected by my family but it didn't worry me because I'd found new friends and a new philosophy.

Life at Elmsett was hard; we had very little money and tried to live off farming the small amount of land that we had. Most of us were urbanites and so found the early mornings, bitter weather in the winter, and punishing physical labour extremely arduous. But I loved it, I loved the arrangements and it was a new life. I had never met such a thing before.

Elmsett was run on an income-pooling basis. The theory was that we would pool all our resources, be they money or books or furniture, everything came into the community, that was the theory. The theory didn't always work out as there were at least two members of the community who were fairly wealthy and it was commonly known that they had money or income of their own. For the rest of us, it was easy, as we had no money. After I left my job, I came to Elmsett with nothing but my books, my papers and my bicycle.

We always appointed a community treasurer, hopefully somebody who could add up, he held the money and there was a community banking account, which he managed on our behalf. If anyone wanted money they had to say what it was for, we then would put it to our weekly council meeting and if it was reasonable we would agree to pay for it. If it were considered frivolous, it would be refused. Clothing expenses, for example, were not reasonable: we wore clothes until they literally dropped off or couldn't be mended by the girls. We didn't buy clothes unless it was absolutely necessary. The clothing we did wear was weird in the extreme. I always wore a blue sleeveless vest with corduroy trousers. I used to cycle around on a trade bike with a five-gallon can in front of me, wearing these garments and people just looked in amazement, they really did.

It was part of our ideal that we should come together twice a day, once for the main meal of the day and the other time for the evening service, which we held in a converted beach hut. We had a big barn at the community in which we had a piano, a long table with a chair at either end and benches such as you might use at school in the gym and we had most of our meals there. Sometimes couples would have tea in their rooms but we always had lunch, we didn't call it lunch, 'our bait' was the word we used; that was always in the barn, all together and visitors, too. The food was pretty awful. We weren't meat eaters, we were all vegetarians and so the food was simple, direct

For 'townies' like Noel, life at Elmsett was hard but rewarding.

but repetitious. We were never hungry because the simple things that we had could be repeated. We made our own bread – we had our own stone mill – we always had oats, because we fed the horses oats, so we could always make oatmeal. So we lived quite well, provided you could put up with a pretty rough diet. You got used to it and I imagine it was far better than army food. Cordon bleu it was not, but people didn't visit the community for what they were going to eat. They visited the community to see what ideas we had on life. Every evening we would have a service led by one of the members. Sometimes it was Christian, sometimes Buddhist, sometimes philosophical or sometimes we would discuss music or poetry. The more dramatic among us put on plays and shows for the local village.

There is no doubt that the village life had continued in the same way for centuries. Never before had they had an influx of young men and one or two women living together, wearing odd clothes and singing hymns to themselves in the field – they'd never met that before and we were a source of great amusement to the villagers. For the first six or seven months, though, the village had been hostile and I was very doubtful at times whether I had done the right thing. After perhaps a year or so, within the community we worked with the village people, they came to understand us even if they didn't agree.

There were certain things that the village and indeed our parents had absolutely no idea about. It's obvious, I suppose, when you were remote from your family, but living with twelve other people, three or four of whom were girls, that relationships would build up and, indeed, they did. Some of us had no inhibitions with regard to relationships, we were thoroughly fed up with the hypocrisy of social life as it went on in town and we were glad to be free to be with whom we wished. The whole community was based on love, we had our poetry written by members of the community, we spoke of love – not in physical terms necessarily, but we would do anything for one another. The fact that some people were sleeping together we accepted, be they a man and a girl or two boys or whatever, provided it wasn't done for purely lustful reasons. It was accepted and wasn't a problem within the community. At the time, the relationships that took place were so taboo that they just wouldn't have been accepted outside. What went on wasn't broadcast abroad, the village people never asked any questions. They knew that we had three caravans, a shepherd's hut, a beach hut and four bedrooms in the house, so if they worked it out for themselves, they must have wondered how we did manage but they never asked.

I arrived at Elmsett with a friend of mine from school, we both rode there on our bicycles, we were both working in insurance at the time, we were both great music lovers, so we had a lot in common. It was just a question of 'well, where's the spare bed for the two new men coming from Ipswich?' and so we slept together from the word go, for practical reasons,

'The whole community was built on love. We would do anything for one another.'

apart from how we might feel. That lasted, well it virtually lasted until I got engaged to my wife, and the fact of having extra girls rather transformed the scene. I wasn't too keen on women, to be perfectly frank, but then I fell in love with a girl who later became my wife. Margaret came to visit the community one day and we simply fell in love. She was so attractive, beautiful, and was a loving and generous soul. It just so happened that at the time Margaret came on the scene another girl also arrived – perhaps it was stars directing our lives in some way, but my friend fell in love with this girl and they too got married.

Not everyone in the community agreed with the freedom of relationships. Sometimes people would use it to their advantage; one fellow was after two girls at the same time to make certain of at least one. When I asked one of the older members for some advice about a relationship between two boys, he was amazed, even though he was living in the community, to think any such thing was occurring. He eventually left as he felt that anyone practising such relationships was being sinful and un-Christian.

Differences of opinion eventually became more and more pronounced. One of the difficulties in running any commune is what people bring to it. Some people brought nothing more than an ability to write poetry, sing songs and play the piano; this enraged the more practical people. More fundamental than that was when I began to realise that, at Elmsett, all the members were very different in their approaches and in what they wanted. As long as these differences prevailed, we would never succeed, either at producing land communities, or overthrowing capitalism or anything else. I would have to look somewhere else to realise my ends and interests. Other members felt the same.

For a while, though, I had been part of a commune movement. At Elmsett I had been involved in exchanges with other communities up and down the land, visiting different places and helping to build a more peaceful society. We went to large cities like Birmingham and Manchester to almost plead with people to come forth and join some of these land communes and see what life could really offer. Yes, we were doing that and of course at times we were successful. People did come to the commune movement.

'Society can grow in a peaceful way.'

Looking back on Elmsett, what I remember more than anything else is the sense of being on the land, in the open air and with the animals. Looking at the stars at night, playing records on the grass at eleven or more at night, walking miles, to meet and talk with people. Even though it didn't work out then, as a result of my experiences at Elmsett I believe that there is a better style of living and that society can grow in a peaceful way.

Dorothy Maclean

I was at university in Ontario, Canada when war broke out and my whole generation then got shot all over the world. I volunteered for wartime work with the British Secret Intelligence Service in New York. When I came to London I was married to an Englishman who was a Sufi. He had educated me in Sufi teachings, which meant that I could accept all religions as leading to the same God within. When I talk about God, I mean the life force in everything and I have always believed in that, even as a child.

Coming to Britain was interesting for me because I found there were spiritual groups which I had not found in Canada or the States and they had been going for quite some time, groups like the White Eagle Lodge and the Order of the Cross. On the whole, I found that Canada was very provincial against the greater knowledge of the world Britain had from her Empire. The ideas of these groups seemed to confirm the sort of beliefs that I felt.

In London I re-met a woman called Sheena, whom I had come across in New York. She became a friend, was a very loving person and gradually became a teacher to me. A group of people formed around Sheena who were trying to make inner contact, and amongst that group were Peter and Eileen Caddy with whom I later went to Findhorn.

I can pinpoint the moment when I had real inner contact. It was a test of love. I loved my husband with a completely possessive love, I was totally dependent on him and I didn't want that. He had been sent to Berlin for work and I was at home in London, desperately lonely and unhappy. One day I was sitting at the table and had a wonderful inner experience when I knew that God was within, I mean the life force in everything, and I knew

Dorothy was born in Ontario, Canada in 1920. As she grew up she was continually seeking a deeper understanding of the meaning of life but was frustrated in finding the answers. During the war she came to London and found herself in a world of people who were exploring new ideas of spirituality. It was here that Dorothy met Peter and Eileen Caddy with whom she later went on to form Findhorn, the first major New Age community in Britain, in the north-east of Scotland. Dorothy structured her days around periods of meditation and receiving guidance on which she acted. It was through this work that she came to believe that she was in contact with spirits of the nature kingdom and learned how to live and work co-operatively with nature. Findhorn became known for its giant vegetables grown on infertile soil. Dorothy returned to the United States in 1973 to found the Lorian community. An extremely active 79 year-old she spends most of the year travelling around the world giving workshops and talks on the knowledge and experiences she gained during her time at Findhorn.

then I was part of a wonderful, harmonious universe, no longer a lonely misfit and that changed
me completely. I had believed in these things
before but now it was a reality, this made all the
difference, and the next day when I saw my
friends they said, 'What's happened to you,
you're different, your voice has changed.' What I
wanted was a truly unconditional love and so I
thought the only way to achieve this was to let
my husband go and divorce him, which I did.

After this, I started living alone and a thought
used to come to me, whenever I was quiet, to
stop, listen and write. I didn't understand and

*Dorothy learned how to respect
and live with plants.*

didn't want that, I thought I might be getting nonsense so I ignored it. Then
one day I got my shorthand notebook and thought, 'I'll listen.' I tried to
think of this wonderful experience I'd had of God and which I thought was
a safe place to be in and I got lovely inspiring thoughts which I wrote down.
I must have told Sheena about this and she said, 'I believe you're getting the
truth, why don't you do what you're asked: stop and write.' She gave me
discipline, because I had no inner discipline to do that.

Sheena was also encouraging a whole group of us to make that inner
contact and to listen within. Eileen Caddy was writing down her guidances
like me. Unfortunately as a group we ran into some trouble and became
rather infamous as the 'Nameless Ones'. A man had left his wife and daughter to become a disciple of Sheena's but the mother-in-law was furious. She
went to the press and said, 'There's this horrible woman who is breaking
up families.' A reporter came to investigate. We thought this a wonderful
opportunity to tell a waiting world the truth and so they interviewed us
and then, when it came out in the papers, it was just really making fun of
us. They didn't understand us. 'Are you Christian?' they'd ask. 'Yes.' 'Are
you Buddhist?' 'Yes.' I mean that was too much. 'Have you got a name?'
'No,' so they called us the 'Nameless Ones' with all the horrible connota-
tions that go with that. Somehow it caught on and there can't have been a
lot of news at the time as it made the papers for months. We had run away
to Scotland by then and were lying low.

By this time I knew that I had to stay with Peter and Eileen Caddy.

Findhorn became famous for its giant vegetables grown on infertile soil.

Eventually Peter got a job running Cluny Hill Hotel, near Forres, and we went with him. That worked out and we were transferred to a hotel in the Trossachs which wasn't a success, so we ended up back in a caravan in Findhorn near the first hotel. It was the only roof that we had at the time. To our astonishment, our inner guidance told us that we must stay there, we tried to get work but couldn't and so we went on the dole. We had very little money so we tried to grow vegetables for extra food and this was the start of the Findhorn garden.

One morning – it was May 1963, I guess – I was told in my meditation that I had a job – to commune with nature – and I thought this would be a wonderful opportunity to go for long walks. I told Peter about this and he said, 'maybe you could help with the garden.' We were having a hard time growing vegetables in the sand. The next day, I tuned in and was told yes, everything in nature had an intelligence and I was to attune to the essence of that intelligence. When I heard this, I immediately argued because how could a vegetable have intelligence, ridiculous, it didn't have a brain, but I was told it wouldn't be so difficult, just stay attuned within and it would work out. By this time, I had had ten years of knowing that it always worked out if you went with it, so sure enough I continued in my meditations and made a breakthrough. I found an intelligence communicating with me.

The first vegetable I chose was the one I love eating most, the garden pea, and I tried to think of what its uniqueness was, what was the essence of this particular plant, its leaves, flower, colour, taste. I tried to focus on the essence and I got a communication. It was saying it wished that human beings wouldn't go about their business the way they did because we're all great beings of light, all we humans, and we aren't using our capabilities. If we did, we could work with them and help the planet. I think that's what nature is trying to say to all of us humans, draw on your Godself, your divinity and then you'll work with us and help the planet.

I was astonished because a vegetable, the garden pea was speaking. But I realised that I wasn't speaking to a plant, I was speaking to the soul level of a species. I didn't have a word for this, to me, it was a formless intelligence, the nearest word I had was angel but that didn't fit as angels have harps and haloes and wings and gold and glitter and this was formless. So I used the word 'deva', which is Sanskrit meaning 'Shining Being' and to me this had no form.

I shared this with Peter and he immediately gave me a list of questions to ask the plants. They never told us what to do but would make suggestions and say, 'this is the nature of the plants' and Peter always followed their suggestions. I remember, for example, we were wondering whether we should plant the watercress in the shade or the sun. The answer was both, so the ones in sun would be ready first and when they were over we could have the ones from the shade. We hadn't thought of that, but it's sensible and an experienced gardener would have known, but we didn't. Most remarkable of all was the change in the soil. I was aware of a presence, which seemed to be in charge of the whole garden, I called it the landscape angel. The landscape angel told me, 'you can't expect us angels to do all the work, you are the ones with hands and feet on the planet, you're the ones on the material plane. You can't expect to have nourishing plants in sand, you have to have nourishing soil and the best thing to do in your particular situation with the sand is to make compost heaps.' So we started to make compost heaps and gradually through the years the sand became soil. Our work with the nature realm meant that we had wonderful plants.

At first, we didn't realise what wonderful plants we had but one day Peter asked a horticultural expert to come and show him how to prune. This expert was

The road sign that greets visitors to Findhorn.

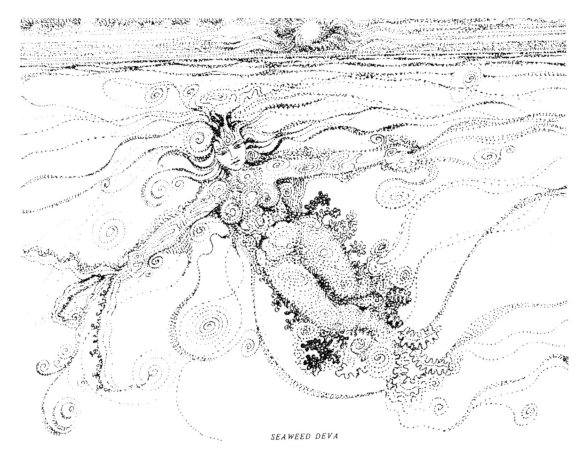

SEAWEED DEVA

amazed at the growth of the vegetables and couldn't believe it was possible in the sandy soil. He asked Peter to come and talk on a BBC radio programme about the garden. Peter didn't dare say that we were communicating with angels and so just put it down to good compost making. Through the BBC, the Soil Association heard about us and Sir George Trevelyan came to visit. He was a follower of Steiner and so we thought he might be sympathetic and he certainly was and he encouraged us to write about it.

When we printed our first book on the Findhorn Garden, we got letters back from all sorts of people saying, 'I thought I was crazy but I've been tuning in to the same sorts of things you have.' It encouraged them to feel better and encouraged us that we weren't complete nuts.

As people came to see the gardens, they realised that we were a small group living according to our spiritual principles and if they were interested they could easily join us. We didn't have any publicity at the beginning but people came from all over the world, with some incredible stories of how the word Findhorn had come to their minds. Somehow, people were drawn and they arrived and we began to grow. We had no intention of being a community, and thank goodness we didn't know, because if we had known we would have thought about it and done all the wrong things, or else we would have run away and said this is ridiculous.

We had no vision of what was going to happen but if we had a problem we could go within and get guidance as to how to deal with it. It always helped us, whether it was a philosophical matter or a practical down-to-earth matter, we could get help from within – nothing is too small to matter.

One day Eileen got guidance that we should have a community centre and I think it was kitchens, which could feed 200 people. At the time, we were only twenty five, so it was crazy and we didn't have any money. But we had learned by then to trust our guidance and also to follow the laws of manifestation. Put briefly that means that if we went in spirit of love and if it was right, then our needs would be met. So it was the right thing to build a community centre, and we built it. The day the kitchen was ready a bill came through the post and, that very same day, somebody donated exactly that amount of money. That sort of thing happened again and again because we were doing what we had been guided to do. People also continued coming to Findhorn and before long the community easily numbered two hundred.

Dorothy now travels the world passing on her Findhorn experience.

After I had been at Findhorn for eleven years, in 1973, I was told that it was time for me to go. At first I resisted, as it was my life and my home but I went within and was told, yes of course it's time to go. Peter didn't believe this and asked Eileen to get guidance, she came back and said, 'Dorothy is quite right, it's time for her to go to her greater work.'

Looking back at my work at Findhorn I now know that it was very important. We have polluted the planet and we are only now realising to what extent. At Findhorn we started dealing with nature in a different way. We've got to change our viewpoint completely and if we can recognise that there's an intelligence we can co-operate with, what a difference it will make to the planet.

THE END
OF TIME

O N the eve of the twentieth century there was a widespread belief that the world was entering a new spiritual age which would bring profound upheaval. The century was first proclaimed to be the Age of Aquarius in 1904 – not in the 1960s, as the hippies believed. Some hoped that this New Age would be one of peace and love, others thought that Armageddon was at hand.

The grim fascination for predicting the end of the world has a long history. Prophecies dating back to Ancient Greece, the Old Testament and more recently to Nostradamus in the sixteenth century have foreseen events leading up to the arrival of the millennium, variously described as the Battle of Armageddon, the Second Coming, or the dawning of the Age of Aquarius. Many of the dates given for these cataclysmic events are in this century. The visionary and magician Aleister Crowley was the first to declare the Age of Aquarius starting in 1904. Mme Blavatsky's Theosophical Society chose 1911 on the basis of words of the Lord Maitreya, the supreme Master, as dictated to Krishnamurti, who was then their World Teacher.

OPPOSITE

Charging a prayer battery on a mountain top. The Aetherius Society believe that mountains are centres of spiritual energy.

In 1931 another visionary, Alice Bailey, received confirmation that the Age of Aquarius had begun.

The outbreak of the First World War, in 1914, was seen by many as confirmation that the Battle of Armageddon was underway. Throughout this century people have interpreted war, natural disasters and the nuclear threat as evidence that the end is imminent. This reached a peak in the sixties and seventies with the growth of a number of religious movements revolving around end-of-time predictions and against a background of 'Ban the Bomb' marches and the hippie declaration of a New Age of love and peace.

There have been two main types of end-of-world movements. The first, influenced by Evangelical thought and a literal interpretation of the Book of Revelations, centres on a Doomsday view of the end of the world with death and destruction. The second movement is more liberal, influenced by Eastern spirituality and envisages a gentle move towards a New Age attained through love and a sharing of the Earth's resources to live in a post-industrial utopia.

The most influential group to have predicted dates for the end of the world are the Jehovah's Witnesses, formerly known as bible students, one of several new religious movements that originated in America during the nineteenth century. In common with the Seventh Day Adventists who predicted the Second Coming for 1844 and the Christadelphians who calculated 1868, the Jehovah's Witnesses promoted a millennium message, that Christ would shortly return and set up his earthly kingdom for a thousand years.

Pastor Russell, the founding father of the Jehovah's Witnesses, first calculated from the Bible that 1874 was the date for the establishment of the Kingdom of God and when this failed he settled upon October 1st 1914. In a series of books, called *Millennial Dawn,* Russell roused his disciples with promises of the kingdom near at hand, and prophesied that 'millions now living will never die.' He preached that there would be 144,000 chosen ones who would be saved after the Battle of Armageddon and go to Heaven and rule with Christ. In 1912 he began work on one of his most ambitious projects, the Photo-Drama of Creation. Through a mixture of slides and moving pictures with sound, ahead of its time, Russell portrayed events from Creation to the end of

Christ's 1000-year reign. Tens of thousands of people saw the film in cinemas and were encouraged to join the bible students.

When the First World War began in August 1914 Russell and his followers saw it as confirmation that the prediction was coming true. In Britain, many bible students gave up their jobs and sold their homes in order to dedicate themselves to spreading the word about the end. They went door to door distributing tracts with Russell's message. Ninety-nine year-old Albert Hudson remembers riding a tram on October 1st, 1914, on what was a beautiful sunny day, and thinking that he must have arrived in Heaven. When the prediction failed to materialise, the Witnesses recalculated the date as first 1918, then 1925, 1940 and 1975. These dates have often coincided with times of national crisis; the 1975 prediction was formulated in the 1960s at the height of the Cold War. Each time the event failed to happen, disappointed followers fell away, but new supporters came along in the build-up to the next date.

In the heady days of the 1960s and '70s when flower power was at its height and the message of the moment was 'Make love not war', the hippie movement popularised the notion of the Age of Aquarius, ushering in a period of earthly love and peace, not of Judgement, war in heaven, salvation and damnation. Eastern gurus were hugely influential in the movement, one of which was Guru Maharaji of the Divine Light Mission. Maharaji was still a small boy in India in the early 1970s when it was announced that he was God returned to Earth to bring in a thousand years of peace. In 1973, he summoned all his followers including several thousand from Britain to go to the Houston Astrodome for Millennium 73, a three-day festival at which he intended to launch the spiritual millennium. Many of the followers expected the end of the world to happen while they were gathered in the Astrodome and visitors to appear from other planets. The event was a financial disaster for the Divine Light Mission with fewer than 144,000 chosen disciples turning up and many of those disillusioned about the non-arrival of the millennium.

Parallel to the nuclear threat of the 1960s and '70s was an increasing awareness of the possibility of life on other planets. The first reported sighting of a flying saucer in 1947 together with the growth of science fiction and NASA's space programme brought the whole universe into the broad picture of events leading to the New Age. Groups started to believe that beings from space might have a role to play in the Millennium. Even Christian organisations like the Mormons were bitten by the UFO bug, allocating other planets as post-Apocalypse repositories for unredeemed souls.

In 1954, a British taxi driver, George King, heard a mysterious voice telling him that he was the spokesman of the 'Interplanetary Parliament'. King received messages from 'cosmic masters' on other planets warning of such terrestrial disasters as hurricanes and earthquakes.

These upheavals in the natural world were thought to herald the new spiritual order which beings like the Master Aetherius from Venus were attempting to bring to earth. King formed the Aetherius Society and, in 1958, received a direct communication from the 'gods from space' which informed him about a Second Coming. The next Master will 'come in a Spacecraft and walk openly among mankind. Unlike previous Interplanetary Masters who have visited this Earth, such as Sri Krishna, the Lord Buddha, the Master Jesus and others, He will not be born through the womb of an Earth woman, but will come in His Full Aspect, or unlimited Being.'

Since then the members of the Aetherius Society have been preparing for the forthcoming New Age. According to them, those not ready for it will be reborn onto another planet. King believed that we have already missed the Apocalypse by a hair's breadth, and have been saved by the work of the Aetherius Society in generating spiritual power to protect the Earth, in particular against nuclear pollution.

The Aetherius Society shares a belief in spiritual masters and rein-carnation with many other Eastern-inspired religious movements including Theosophy. Benjamin Creme is one New Age prophet who believes in the living spiritual hierarchy of Masters and that Jesus, Bud-dha, Krishna and the other great religious teachers were Masters.

Creme believes he was contacted by a Master in 1959 and told of a Second Coming, that Maitreya, the supreme Master, would return to Earth imminently. Creme heard nothing more until the early 1970s when he claimed to receive further messages and heard from Maitreya himself. Maitreya's message was simple: 'Share and Save the World.' In 1982, Creme announced that Maitreya was living anonymously in the Asian community in the East End of London and would reveal himself to the world shortly. Since then, it is claimed he has made a number of appearances including one at a healing meeting in Nairobi in June 1988. These appearances are all a prelude to the Day of Declaration when Maitreya will appear on radio and television all over the world and speak to everyone, telepathically, in their own language.

Inevitably, the year 2000 is now the focus for all the millennial groups, both evangelical and New Age. One of Nostradamus' most spe-cific quatrains said, 'In the year 1999, in the seventh month, a great and terrible Lord will come from the sky, reviving the great King of the Mongols – before and after his coming Mars will reign happily.' Recent natural events like the disturbance in climate caused by El Niño and the presence of the Hale-Bopp comet in 1997 have been interpreted as mil-lennial signs. In California, one group called Heaven's Gate celebrated the appearance of the comet by committing suicide. According to them, the comet was 'the marker we've been waiting for, the time for the arrival of the spacecraft from the Level of Human to take us home to 'Their World', in the literal heavens.'

So far in Britain there have not been such dramatic events, but those who had been let down by the millennial predictions of their groups often faced harsh treatment. Jehovah's Witnesses who questioned the validity of the dates for Armageddon were dis-fellowshipped and shunned by their friends and family in the movement. Divine Light Mis-sion members who chose to leave were told that they would go mad.

Albert Hudson

I was at a meeting in 1913 where a lot of people around the table were enthusing about what was going to happen the following October. They said that the chosen ones would be miraculously taken up to heaven and the world would immediately be engulfed in a great war which would lead to the toppling of all the crowned heads of Europe and the collapse of America into a state of communism which in turn would plunge the world into a maelstrom of anarchy. That would lead to a complete breakdown of the present world order and, from then on, there would be the Millennium, the thousand year-reign of Christ over the Earth, in which all forms of iniquity and lawlessness as well as death and disease would be abolished.

It seemed incredible to me that Armageddon would happen and the world could change into another world quite so quickly and so I piped up, 'suppose it doesn't happen?' There was a look of horror around the table and one man said, 'of course, it will happen.' The idea that, within the year, I would see my parents suddenly disappear seemed too quick a transformation.

I went round door to door putting tracts through letter boxes. Everybody was doing it, housewives, even children. It was a daily occupation, everyone gave as much time as they could to the work. They were given maps of local districts and allotted their own section. The pamphlets had an optimistic message of hope and cheerfulness rather than the reverse: the rule of man was coming to an end with a certain amount of disruption but then the change would lead to a much better condition of things. The changeover was going to be relatively quick. Most people accepted the material; it was rare that we had someone throw it away.

The end was coming in October of 1914 and it would start with a disastrous war between the nations. Well, you can imagine what the newspapers made of that, they'd derided it all the way through and Pastor Russell had been saying it for thirty years. But on August 4th this country declared

Albert was born in 1899 in Deptford, London, the eldest of five children. His father was an official on the railways and the family were bible students, forerunners of the Jehovah's Witnesses. The Hudsons, like many bible students at the time, were expecting the world to end on October 1st, 1914. They spent months beforehand going door to door with leaflets warning people of impending Armageddon. The outbreak of the First World War was seen as confirmation that the end was coming. When the event failed to materialise, Albert left college, trained as an engineer and went to work in a telecommunications factory. He lives with his wife Marjorie near Sherborne in Dorset.

*Pastor Russell promised that
144,000 chosen ones would survive the Battle of Armageddon.*

war on Germany and before many months were out the whole world
was at war. What can you say? People had to admit that the prediction
was right after all. There was a certain amount of jubilation amongst the
bible students.

People started getting ready. I knew one accountant in London who gave
up his business to tell everybody what was happening, expecting he could
live for a few months on his earnings and then all the problems would be
solved. I knew another man who was a miner in Nottinghamshire. He was
so certain that he sold his pit boots and all the accoutrements of his job in
expectation.

I was riding to college on an open top tram – it was a beautiful day with
a brilliant blue sky and the sun was shining in the way it rarely does in October. The tram went alongside a belt of woods and I noticed that all the trees
were green, greener than they ought to be in October. I remember distinct-
ly saying, 'they were right after all, it has happened, this can't be the old
world – it shouldn't be like this in October, this must be the Millennium.'
I went to my studies considerably heartened and told all the other lads that

ABOVE
Bible students during the 1910s.

BELOW
Albert and Marjorie Hudson in their garden near Sherborne.

"WHAT PASTOR RUSSELL SAID"

What does the Word say?   *Well···I would say···*   *What do YOU say?*

the Millennium was starting. They'd heard me talking about it before, some believed it and others were rather sarcastic about it.

My mother was disappointed when Armageddon didn't happen. People found that they didn't have jobs to go back to, but then the message changed and we were told that it would happen later – in 1918. For my part, I had no faith in 1918; by this time, I was beginning to develop a spirit of enquiry into things that had been absent when I was younger. Quite a few of us became disillusioned and left. I rejected a great deal by the time I was in my twenties. After 1918 failed to happen, they predicted the end for 1925 but by that time I'd broken away.

155

Syd Hancock

Maharaji was just a young boy, a remarkable child. After his father's death he was proclaimed as the new guru. He spoke with great authority, great conviction, in front of large crowds. In 1970, when he was only 13 years old, he had a big open-air meeting in New Delhi called the Peace Bomb when he said he had come to bring peace to the world, and that in every age when the planet is in great turmoil, the Lord will come in human form to draw his true devotees to him and lead them to the path of righteousness. So he was presenting himself as the one to save the planet.

Syd Hancock was born in 1951 and grew up in Cornwall, the elder of two brothers. His father was a Methodist preacher and his mother was the local schoolteacher. Aged 20, Syd embarked on a spiritual path seeking the answers to questions about the meaning of life which he hadn't found in Christianity. In the early 1970s he dropped out, experimented with drugs and discovered Eastern spirituality at the same time as the Beatles. Syd set off for India, the spiritual capital of the world, but never got any farther than Leicester where he discovered the young guru of the Divine Light Mission. Maharaji had said that the millennium was coming in 1973 and that this would mark the end of life as we knew it. All the followers from around the world were encouraged to gather in the Houston Astrodome for Millennium 73, a three-day event where they awaited the dawning of the New Age. Syd was one of those waiting.

He came first to Britain in 1971. I remember seeing pictures of him in the papers when he arrived at Heathrow, there was a real buzz about him. He was at one of the first Glastonbury Festivals, apparently there were coloured lights in the sky when he arrived on stage. It was claimed by the devotees that it was fulfilment of an ancient prophecy that Christ would return and go to Glastonbury.

I was a spiritual seeker and Maharaji had a huge impact then in the community of seekers. I was just 20/21. I'd been searching for spiritual answers for a long time but I was looking beyond the Christian church. I was into some of the ideas of the psychedelic movement, and going beyond the mind into higher consciousness using psychedelic drugs. I experimented and discovered realms of consciousness and experiences beyond the everyday. Once I'd had those experiences, I knew there was more to life than mundane everyday experiences. I wasn't alone, I decided to leave behind the drugs and find that kind of higher consciousness within myself. I started discovering other religions, got interested in other ideas, the Beatles had come across the Maharashi, so meditation and yoga had become mainstream.

One of the things that attracted me to Maharaji is that he said that God is an experience and not just words in a book. He said that he could reveal to me how to have a personal inner experience of God. I'd gone to visit friends in Leicester before I set off for India looking for a guru, and I saw a poster for the Divine Light Mission. There's an old teaching that when you're ready for something, it comes to you and that was certainly the case. I thought maybe the guru has come here to me and I don't need to go to India.

That was January, 1973. I ended up living in an ashram, meditating regularly. I was really obsessed with telling people about the Knowledge, the meditation techniques of Divine Light Mission, fund-raising and spreading Maharaji's message. We would tell friends, stop people on the street, give out leaflets. The atmosphere was euphoric, heightened. People were starting to believe that Maharaji was God come back in human form to bring world peace

Syd Hancock discovered Eastern spirituality in his early twenties.

and he'd said it was going to happen very soon. There was an ecological awareness, then, that we were destroying the planet with poisons, nuclear power was dangerous and something had to be done. The feeling was growing that if we continued like this it was going to mean wholesale destruction throughout the world unless we reversed things. That was one of the threads of the pre-millennial feeling that was developing. I remember once having an LSD trip when I walked out of Leicester into the hills and I was looking down on the city. As I was watching it seemed to shimmer and disappear, it felt very real to me and I thought, 'Oh gosh, it's gone, that's it, civilisation's ended now, we'll have to start all over again.' Other times, I'd be walking through the streets and thinking that all around me would be derelict soon, creepers would grow, and it would go back to nature.

The premies, the followers of Maharaji, were galvanised, it was impossible to ignore the message. Out of my friends, I was the first to join. My family thought it was just the excesses of youth. We believed that the *Book of Revelations* was coming true. There's going to be 144,000 of us, we're the chosen ones; the world is going to end and Maharaji's going to bring in the Kingdom of Heaven. In that fervour you really wanted everyone to be there with you, so we bombarded people with stuff, it was a very intense time.

It was announced that Maharaji's biggest festival in the West to date was going to take place in November in Houston, U.S.A. It was called Millennium 73. People from all over the West and India were encouraged to go. This was going to be where Maharaji would announce his plan to bring peace to the world. It was called the Millennium Festival because it was going to inaugurate a thousand years of peace, the Age of Aquarius was going

to come in and the world was going to end. There was also a comet, Kohoutek, that was going to blaze across the sky as another sign to usher in the New Age. Maharaji said that when they gathered in the Astrodome the air would be filled with petals, rose petals fall from the sky and angels sing. In the build-up beforehand in the magazines, it was said that the sky would be full of flying saucers because all the beings of the universe were coming to Maharaji.

People were going from all around the world. We were told, 'You must go there, you must be on the plane.' Three planes were chartered from Heathrow to go to Houston. I was on the second plane but I remember standing on an observation deck watching the first plane leave. I was leaving behind my family and friends and we weren't coming back, we were going to Heaven, we weren't going to see this place or those people ever again. I felt that we had tried our best to get them to come and we could not have done any more.

On arrival in Houston we stayed in a big hotel and went to the Festival everyday. I can remember looking at the sky for the comet and being very excited. Actually in the Astrodome were far fewer than the 144,000 who were expected. I remember seeing large tables of food left to rot. Maharaji sat on a big ornate throne on a big stage with huge video screens behind him showing flower children and student protests, that sort of thing. There were rock bands playing. The message in the music and pictures was that this was what we'd lived through: all this struggle leading up to this moment. Maharaji had a programme of talks which he gave every evening about how he was going to bring peace to the world. There was so much euphoria, it was quite dislocated from reality, there wasn't a fearful feeling of the world coming to an end.

When we came to the end of the event and it didn't happen, some people felt let down, especially those political activists who had taken it all very literally. I was one of the many who felt that these things happen on the inside, our experience of the world had changed on the inside, but not necessarily on the outside. As an inner experience, we felt the world had ended; the world would never be the same again. It was a very deep thing.

'After Houston, I devoted my life to serving Maharaji and followed the vows of poverty, chastity and obedience.'

I returned to Britain and renounced the world. I devoted my life to serving Maharaji and gave up worldly goods, desire for a career and followed the vows of poverty, chastity and obedience. The euphoria died down after Millennium 73. Although people didn't necessarily feel let down, the intensity had gone. I was living in an ashram but after a year I started questioning what I was doing, why I was giving up the world when I barely had any experience of it. I was still in my early twenties. I eventually decided to go and try the world, and thought that I could always go back but I drifted away, and never did return.

Ray Nielsen

Ray was born in 1936. He grew up in London and his earliest memories are of looking out of his bedroom window during the Blitz. He first encountered the Aetherius Society in 1960, and came to believe in the existence of Masters from other planets. Through what he describes as his cosmic experiences, he feels he has found proof of the work of George King, the founder of the Aetherius Society. King claimed to have received over 600 messages from Masters on other planets delivering spiritual teachings and communications of hope. In 1958, King received a message that there would soon be a Second Coming, the dawning of a New Age and that the Lord would arrive in a spacecraft from another planet. Ray's dedication to George King and the Aetherius Society has taken him around the world, both on individual missions and eventually for a longer period of time to the United States where he worked at the Aetherius headquarters. He has recently returned from the States and is now working for a company that has links with the Society. He is in a constant state of preparation for the coming of the New Age.

I was born in 1936 in north London and I was there during the bombing. The atmosphere during the Blitz was quite terrifying for a boy of six or seven years of age. We lived in a house overlooking a park and I used to lie awake at night, looking out at the bombs falling and the search lights and hearing all the machine guns and screams. I used to try and detach myself from this by looking at the stars; I had a particularly beautiful view of the Big Dipper from my bedroom window and I used to watch this night after night. I used to think about what life must be like out there and are they going through this type of experience? Then one morning I got up very early, which is unusual for me – there was a little hole in the fence opposite the house where we used to go into the park. I went into the park, the wind was blowing and I kicked the leaves with my feet. Then I heard a voice, very, very plainly in my head. It said to me that this was a phase that would disappear and I would grow up. Eventually, I would meet a very special person. This person would have a very important role to play as far as the world was concerned. This occurred when I was still a boy and, after the war, I forgot about the incident and life went on.

I went to school and then into the Royal Navy, where I did my national service. I got married at the age of 21 and we moved to Palmers Green, north London. At that time I was playing in a jazz group in Hampstead, two or three nights a week, and I had a day job. One morning on my way to work, I looked down the tube – I know that this sounds strange – and I saw a young man there, he looked at me and it was the most extraordinary experience, because I knew this person from a previous life. I've always believed in reincarnation without even reading about it or being told about it. I've always felt that I'd lived before. To cut a long story short, we met, we discussed our lives and where we were living. We lived very close to each other and he was a musician. It just so happened that I needed another musician to join my group and so he did. In a few weeks we became good friends. We played in this club in Hampstead and one night he asked me if I believed in reincarnation and I said, 'Yes,' and he said, 'Well, do you believe in Cosmic Masters?' I looked at him with an almost explosive reaction because I felt this was leading to something very important and he then told me about the Aetherius Society.

George King, founder of the Aetherius Society: in touch with cosmic masters.

He had come across the Aetherius Society and met the leader, George King, who claimed to be in contact with Cosmic Masters. I didn't reject it, I found myself almost wanting then and there to rush to the Aetherius Society and find out more. I went home and told my wife, who was raised as a Catholic, I was a bit concerned as to how she would take it, but we discussed it and she felt that it was important for me to find out more about this. So I went along to the Aetherius Society headquarters on the Fulham Road, walked in and then I remembered the incident as a young boy. I felt that I had arrived.

At that very first meeting, I was a bit disappointed as George King had just left for America. But they played me what they described as a transmission. It was a tape recording of an actual message that came through to King while he was in very deep yogic trance. Now I'd never read a book on metaphysics before, I'd never read a book on trance, mediumship or anything, but when they played that transmission to me – it was a transmission from one of the Cosmic Masters – I felt a vibration from the very tip of my toe to the top of my head. It was extraordinary. I just knew that this was the voice of an intelligence that was far, far more advanced than anybody on this earth. It had the authority and it had some essence very difficult to describe. I began to study the transmissions. In a very short space of time I became a member. I was accepted as a student and had the privilege of working with George King for the next thirty-seven years.

I had absolutely no trouble in accepting that there was intelligent life on other planets. Historically, it made absolute sense. How do you explain the extraordinary people who have been on Earth, Krishna, the Lord Buddha,

the Master we call Jesus, St Peter, to mention just a few? They all refer to higher beings that have contacted them or left them with higher teachings. Also, for me, I felt that I had experienced something. If you experience something it is no longer a question of belief, it's a question of being part of it. I found tremendous strength when I came up against opposition. I always used to say that it is easy to criticise, it doesn't take any effort at all, but to investigate something takes a little bit more energy. But it's far more profitable in the long run because when you do investigate something then you get right to the heart of it, and you open yourself up to a greater awareness. My friends and family were the ones who had difficulty in accepting this. Many of my friends were very sceptical about the whole thing and we parted company. As I became dedicated to the Aetherius Society, I spent more and more time there, my wife accepted this and soon we moved from north London to Fulham so that we could be near the headquarters. Eventually I worked there full time.

In the early days of the Society the main urgency was to get the message out about the danger of atomic experimentation. The transmissions that were coming from the Cosmic Masters were increasing in intensity and in nature. Of course, you've got to remember that, in those days, the Cold War tension had gripped the world like an iron vice and the nuclear question was extremely worrying for people. So a lot of our work was to get the message out, hold public meetings, go on radio and television and write articles. The society was growing quite rapidly, we would have classes and courses to attract people and I remember going to places like Cambridge University and to groups who were treating the subject of UFOs in a sort of half-hearted way. Our message was that we were not a flying saucer organ-

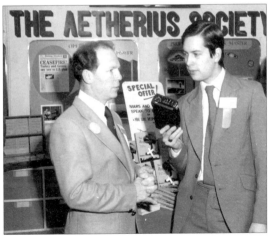

TOP
Ray Nielsen displays the flying saucer model to a lecture audience.

BOTTOM
Ray (left) at the 1979 Mind, Body, Spirit festival at Olympia, London.

isation but more interested in the reason why flying saucers were here. At that time, despite all the Government and military denials, thousands of people had seen UFOs, there was intense cosmic activity as the threat of nuclear disaster was real.

The experience of actually witnessing flying saucers from other worlds has been quite extraordinary. I've been very fortunate to have had many such experiences. I remember one particularly extraordinary sighting. It was a cloudless night. I was standing on the top of Holdstone Down and saw space craft going from one side of the horizon to the other in seconds. Not only that, they were also going in zigzag formations, they were doing curvatures, they were doing figures of eight. I've seen spacecraft go in one direction, stop, and go immediately in the opposite direction, but here was a display that was absolutely unbelievable, except it was actually happening. Lots of people ask me, 'How come you've seen these craft and I haven't?' I also ask them a question, 'Have you ever looked?' You'd be surprised at how few people have actually taken the time to study the sky – just look at the skies because spacecraft are there, there's no question about it.

One of the missions that was performed between 1958 and 1961 was called Operation Starlight. This involved certain mountains around the world being chosen as New Age power centres. The mountains would be charged and the energy would be stored there, for people to tap. Nineteen mountains were chosen and George King was used as a terrestrial anchor to channel the energy. He had to go to each of the mountains around the world and act as a channel for the cosmic energy. I was invited to go as part of the support team on one of these missions. The cosmic intelligences revealed which mountain would be charged and we went and camped at the base for two or three nights. On the third morning, very early, we went up the mountain for George King to receive the initial charge. Thinking back over it, it was one of the most extraordinary experiences of my life. During the actual charge, I felt so close to the truth, I felt that this is what life is all about. I felt a tremendous closeness, a spiritual awakening. It was more real and made more sense than anything I have experienced in the physical world. It remains with me to this day, it gave me a sense of my true being, that we're here on this planet to realise our spiritual potential and at that moment I was given a glimpse of what my spiritual self was really like. I think that if everybody were able to tap into that and to live with that spiritual potential actually manifesting twenty-four hours a day, we would have the New Age in a very, very short space of time.

The Aetherius Society's teachings indicate that a New Age of enlightenment will take place on this earth. When George King was performing Operation Starlight he received a very definite message that there would be another coming, another Master would come to this earth to lead people into the New Age. This Master will not be born through the womb again but will actually land. This means that he will use a spacecraft of some description. We believe it will be a definite event when everybody will know and there'll be no doubt about it. He will identify himself and will approach world leaders and state who he is, where he comes from and what his mission is. His main purpose will be to lead those who are ready into the New Age. Not everyone is going to be ready for the New Age and those who are not ready will leave this realm of existence and go to another planet. They will be reborn on a younger world in order to re-live their history and go through the same experiences again. The New Age will only be peopled by those who are ready. We consider this to be a definite cosmic statement and it's tantamount to the sorting of the wheat from the chaff. No date has been given for the start of the New Age for the simple reason that mankind is being given the opportunity to prepare for it through the messages of the Cosmic Masters. If this New Age is brought in gradually, then more and

'Those not ready for the New Age will go to another planet.'

more people will not only learn about it but will be ready for it. Mankind has freewill and it is up to us all to accept the knowledge of the coming of the New Age consciously and willingly through our inner realisation.

I believe that those of us who have been with the Aetherius Society, and have had the privilege of George King's leadership, are ready for the New Age. We look forward to it with great humility and great reverence because this will signify the beginning of a new era, not only for us, but for every living soul on this earth who is ready for this new experience.

Benjamin Creme

It was while I was growing up in Glasgow that I first came across the Masters in books by Madame Blavatsky and Alice Bailey. They are people like us who are ahead of us in evolution – advanced, perfected beings. They've come to the end of this long, apparently endless evolutionary journey on which all of us are engaged and they live in remote mountain and desert areas like the Himalayas from where they have overseen the evolution of humanity from the earliest times. If you look at humanity as a whole, you will see that there's a graduation from the youngest soul living now on Earth up to the most advanced being who is the Christ himself, the Lord Maitreya, to give him his personal name, who is the World Teacher at the head of that group of masters connected with human evolution.

Benjamin Creme was born in Glasgow in 1922 and studied art, later becoming a painter in the modernist style. Through the esoteric writings of Mme Blavatsky and Alice Bailey he came to believe in the existence of the 'Masters of Wisdom', a group of superior wise beings who have evolved through many incarnations and live in remote parts of the world. They are the custodians of the 'Divine Plan' for this planet. In 1959 Benjamin believes he was contacted by one of the Masters who told him that Maitreya, the Supreme Master, the Messiah of all religions would return to live in the everyday world during the 1970s and that this would be the Second Coming, heralding a peaceful New Age. Benjamin is Maitreya's roving ambassador travelling the world creating a climate of expectancy for His emergence through the organisation Share International. Maitreya is said to be living anonymously in the Brick Lane area of the East End of London, working in an Indian restaurant.

There are Masters living on all the planets of our solar system. Not at the physical level. If you were to go to Mars, Venus or Jupiter you would see nobody at all, but they're teeming with life on the etheric plan. When those Masters come into our planetary system they come to do special work. They mop up an enormous amount of the pollution and nuclear radiation in our atmosphere. We owe them an enormous debt; the engineers who are from Mars have placed around this planet a ring of light which keeps it intact in its axis. They mop up with implosion devices much of the pollution which we pour into the world, especially nuclear pollution. The Masters see pollution as the number one killer of this planet and that's what they warn us about.

In 1945, at the end of the war, the Lord Maitreya, the Supreme Master of all religions – Christ to the Christians, Mahdi to the Muslims, the Messiah to the Jews and Krishna to the Hindus – announced his decision to return to the world at the earliest possible moment and to bring His group of Masters out into the world with him. They had been hidden away in the mountains and deserts of the world for one hundred thousand years, near enough. They would come to inaugurate the New Age, the Age of Aquarius as we call it, which would be a tremendous expansion of consciousness for humanity and to inspire us to change the conditions for our everyday life, to make that new civilisation and bring world peace and harmony.

My own inkling of this came in 1958 when I had my first personal contact with a Master. A man came to my door and said that I was receiving communications from the Masters. I said, 'No, I'm not.' He said, 'Oh, yes, you are and I've come to tell you that you are.' I said I hadn't heard a thing but I knew it was a telepathic rapport that they set up with a disciple and I'd had nothing of the kind. I believed in their existence, but I was not expecting any form of communication, nothing could have been further from my mind, but this man said, 'Well, the Masters are sending messages but they just bounce off you because you're not open. Don't worry, it'll come.'

Benjamin Creme: learned about the Masters of Wisdom through the writings of Madame Blavatsky.

After about three months, in March 1959, I had the most extraordinary experience of my life. A tremendous spiritual energy descended from the top of my head and down through my whole body and I began to shake, my heart sort of melted and turned over. I was filled with the love of all the world, it was total bliss. Then I had a vision, it was as if I was inside a great sphere of white light and to the right of me I was looking at all the events of the future and all of this was taking place simultaneously. Maitreya said, 'I, Myself, am coming.' I was taken aback. I thought it would be another Being coming back, another World Teacher and He'd probably come from Venus, I didn't think it would be Maitreya Himself. He said 'I, Myself, am coming, sooner than anyone thinks possible. It will be in about twenty years.' And then He said, 'You'll have a role to play in My coming if you accept it.'

Nothing happened for many years and the subject was dropped until the early 1970s when my Master began to train me to prepare the way for Maitreya and the other Masters to return to the world. Their way needs to be prepared so that they can enter our lives without infringing on our human free will. My job was to create the climate of hope, of expectancy for their coming.

In July 1977, Maitreya descended from his mountain eighteen and a half thousand feet up in the Himalayas, stayed some days on the plains in Pakistan to acclimatise the body which he had been creating for five to six years before that time, found that it was perfectly built, and took a plane that landed in London on July 19th, 1977. He is still a member of the Asian community of London. He has been there ever since that time, first in the

According to Benjamin Creme, Maitreya was seen in Nairobi on June 11th 1988.

*'I was told to hold a press
conference to announce the
coming of the Messiah.'*

Brick Lane area of London. In the beginning, He took a job in a hospital as
a night porter, but He doesn't eat, he doesn't sleep, He works every second of the 24 hours of the day, He can appear and disappear at will, He can
change his appearance at will, He can be a woman or child.

I'd been told that He hoped to make himself known at the very earliest opportunity and hopefully the date would be May 30th, 1982 because that was the Festival of Pentecost and it would be that day because it would be this Pentecostal experience, this time for the whole of humanity, the Declaration. In January I said to my Master, I don't see any sign of Maitreya even in the Asian community, I don't hear Him talked about, let alone enough for the world to be able to come forward. He said, 'Don't worry, we have a contingency plan and that's you.' I was told to hold a press conference. Leading up to it we raised money and spent something like $250,000 on full-page advertisements in some twenty newspapers around the world saying that Christ was about to appear to the world in a few months.

I held my press conference in Los Angeles. All the major TV networks of America were there plus the BBC, on a satellite link from London. I challenged the media of the world to choose a few representatives to come to London and look for Maitreya, and if they did this at a sufficient level, and assigned to the task sufficient clout to be believed, Maitreya would come forward to them. It was a very busy time, there were journalists everywhere, but none of them had sufficient clout for Maitreya. But I'm told his Emergence is now imminent, as soon as the stock markets in the West undergo the collapse which they have already done in the East, Maitreya will come forward to mitigate the effect of this collapse and to show us how to reconstruct our economic world along better ways.

Benjamin Creme: 'Maitreya will appear on television all over the world and speak to everyone in their own language.'

Maitreya has appeared and disappeared several times, as a prelude to the Day of Declaration when He will appear on radio and television all over the world and speak to everyone telepathically in their own language. On that Day humanity will have the most profound, moving experience it has ever had. He no longer needs intermediaries, religious groups, to take his teachings and distort his teachings. He can speak directly to every human being.

FURTHER READING

Ashe, Geoffrey	*The Avalonian Quest*	London, Book Club Associates, 1983
Barrett, David	*Sects, Cults & Alternative Religions*	London, Blandford, 1996
Bloom, William	*The New Age*	London, Rider, 1991
Campbell, Eileen & Brennan, J.H.	*The Aquarian Guide to the New Age*	London, Thorsons, 1990
	Diggers & Dreamers, The Guide to Communal Living	Winslow, Bucks, D & D Publications, 1995
Crowley, Vivianne	*Wicca, The Old Religion in the New Millennium*	London, Thorsons, 1996
Crowther, Patricia	*One Witch's World*	London, Robert Hale, 1998
Heelas, Paul	*The New Age Movement*	Oxford, Blackwell Publishers Ltd, 1996
Hudson, A.O.	*Bible Students in Britain*	Hounslow, Bible Fellowship Union, 1989
Jordan, Michael	*Cults, Prophecies, Practices & Personalities*	1996

King, George with Lawrence, Richard	*Contacts with the Gods from Space, Pathway to the New Millennium*	Los Angeles, 1996
Lamond, Frederic	*Religion without Beliefs*	London, Janus Publishing Company 1997
Michell, John	*The New View Over Atlantis*	London, Thames and Hudson Ltd, 1983
Nelson, G.K.	*Spiritualism and Society*	London, Routledge and Kegan Paul, 1969
Nuttall, Jeff	*Bomb Culture*	London, MacGibbon & Kee, 1968
Parker, Derek & Julia	*A History of Astrology*	London, Andre Deutsch, 1983
Pickstone, Charles	*For Fear of the Angels*	London, Hodder & Stoughton, 1996
Puttick, Elizabeth	*Women in New Religions*	Basingstoke, Macmillan Press, 1997
Robertson, Olivia	*The Call of Isis*	London, Neptune Press, 1975
Shaw, Eva	*Eve of Destruction*	Los Angeles, Lowell House, 1995
Sheridan, Gilley & Sheils, W.J.	*A History of Religion in Britain*	Oxford, Basil Blackwell Ltd, 1994
Singer, Andre & Lynette	*Divine Magic, The world of the supernatural*	London, Boxtree, 1995
Skinner, Stephen	*Millennium Prophecies*	London, Virgin Books, 1994
Slade, Paddy	*Seasonal Magic, The Diary of a Village Witch*	Chieveley, Capall Bann Publishing, 1997
Spencer, Colin	*The Heretic's Feast, A History of Vegetarianism*	London, Fourth Estate Ltd, 1993

Thacker, Joy	*Whiteway Colony, The Social History of a Tolstoyan Community*	Stroud, Sutton Publishing, 1993
Thomas, Terence	*The British, Their Religious Beliefs and Practices 1800-1986*	London, Routledge, 1988
Thompson, Damian	*The End of Time*	London, Minerva, 1997
Valiente, Doreen	*An ABC of Witchcraft Past and Present*	London, Robert Hale, 1996
Washington, Peter	*Madame Blavatsky's Baboon*	Secker & Warburg, 1993

ACKNOWLEDGEMENTS

We would like to thank all the people who have helped us in writing this book and making the television series it accompanies, with special thanks to Peter Grimsdale and Michael Jackson for their belief in the project.

We are also grateful to the other members of the Testimony Films team, especially to the editor Daniel de Waal and also to Andy Attenburrow, Hilary Jelbert, Mary Parsons, Richard van Emden, Mike Humphries, Madge Reed, the cameramen Steve Haskett, Mike Pharey and Dave Blackman and the sound recordists Jeff John and David Harcombe.

We would like to thank John Sansom for his skill in turning this book around in so short a time and Monique Lentier for proof reading the manuscript.

For their advice and support, we are grateful to William Bloom, Bob Gilbert, Nick Campion, The Library of Avalon, Bristol Central Library, the BBC Bristol library, Lyn Guest de Swarte of *Psychic News*, Duncan Gascoigne of the SNU, Prof. Ronald Hutton of Bristol University, Findhorn Foundation, Sunfield School, The Pagan Federation, Jan Faull and the staff of the National Film and Television Archive, Emma Gleadall, Ruby Haslam, Jean and Leslie Laycock, Ros Belford, Alison Shipley, Shona Harris, Melissa Montgomery, Miranda Steed, Sarah Forrest, Zoë Wanamaker, the Bristol Theosophical Society, the Atlantis Bookshop and Justin Toper.

Finally and most importantly, we wish to thank all the contributors to this project who kindly lent us their memories and photographs.

PICTURE CREDITS